From German Cavalry Officer to Reconnaissance Pilot

The World War I History, Memories, and
Photographs of Leonhard Rempe, 1914–1921

Paul L. Rempe

To: Al Jones
Hope you
enjoy this book!
Best wishes
Paul

SB
Savas Beatie
California

First edition, first printing

Library of Congress Cataloging-in-Publication Data

Names: Rempe, Leonhard, 1893-1956, author. | Rempe, Paul Leonhard, editor.
Title: From German Cavalry Officer to Reconnaissance Pilot: the World War I History, Memories, and Photographs of Leonhard Rempe, 1914-1921 / edited by Paul L. Rempe.
Description: First edition. | El Dorado Hills, California: Savas Beatie LLC, 2015. | Includes bibliographical references and index.
Identifiers: LCCN 2015041616| ISBN 9781611213218 (alk. paper) | ISBN 9781940669540 (ebk.)
Subjects: LCSH: Rempe, Leonhard, 1893-1956. | World War, 1914-1918—Personal narratives, German. | World War, 1914-1918—Cavalry operations, German. | World War, 1914-1918—Aerial operations, German. | Soldiers—Germany—Biography.
Classification: LCC D640 .R446 2015 | DDC 940.4/4943092—dc23
LC record available at http://lccn.loc.gov/2015041616

SB

Published by
Savas Beatie LLC
989 Governor Drive, Suite 102
El Dorado Hills, CA 95762
Phone: 916-941-6896
(E-mail) sales@savasbeatie.com

Digital version by Savas Publishing

eISBN: 978-1-94066-954-0

Savas Beatie titles are available at special discounts for bulk purchases in the United States by corporations, institutions, and other organizations. For more details, please contact Special Sales, P.O. Box 4527, El Dorado Hills, CA 95762. You may also e-mail us at sales@savasbeatie.com, or click over for a visit to our website at www.savasbeatie.com for additional information.

All photographs courtesy of the Rempe Family Collection

To my parents,
who taught their children to live in the present, but learn from the past.

Contents

Acknowledgments

This work would not exist were it not for significant help and good counsel from a number of individuals. I am very grateful to them all for their knowledge and their kindness.

Of course, my first debt is to my father, who left Germany for the United States in 1923 but who had the foresight to pack not only clothes but also war-related papers and photographs for the 1914–21 period.

Dr. Dieter H. M. Gröschel, MD played a critical role in recognizing the importance of those archival materials. A medical doctor, Dr. Gröschel's deep interest and understanding of this critical period in German history represents more than an avocation. In this case, Dr. Gröschel carried out a significant amount of research using German sources and thereby confirmed much of my father's experiences in the Great War. Dr. Gröschel also identified many of the individuals in the photographs my father had preserved in his "war album."

The major work of translating my father's papers was undertaken by Dr. Kimberly Redding. Dr. Redding chairs the Department of History at Carroll University and also teaches courses in German history. A valuable colleague while I worked there, I remain grateful for her help. Dr. Michael Koch, of the Language Department at Carroll, also provided some translating help.

Richard Bennett, past President of The League of World War One Aviation Historians, provided valuable information about the German Air Force in general and about my father's units in particular, both during the war and with the Freikorps. He also read an early draft of this work and provided very helpful comments.

I'm also in debt to my student assistant Nate Corvette, and to Kathy Olsen for their help in moving my father's photos into the digital world. Kathy is one of those people associated with Carroll University who provided constant encouragement during the course of this work. Others in the same category include Professor Wis Guthrie and Lance Herdegen, a respected author in his own right on the Civil War in general, and the Union Iron Brigade in particular. Mr. Herdegen has worked with Mr. Theodore P. Savas, Managing Director of Savas Beatie LLC, and I can only agree with Lance Herdegen that Ted Savas is an exceptional publisher. Mr. Savas has provided help and support throughout this project. Along with Mr. Savas, I'm grateful for the editorial suggestions of Mr. Bogdanovic, a keen-eyed editor who makes his home in the United Kingdom.

Finally, I wish to thank my wife, Kathleen, who not only spared me some household chores but provided IT support throughout. Our three sons, Tim, Jon, and Ben motivated me to continue whenever they asked me to tell them stories about the grandfather they never met.

Of course, any and all errors in either text or in mislabeling photographs are mine alone, and I take responsibility for the same.

Introduction

*I*t is difficult to assign a fitting name to the 1914–18 war. It defied all reason then as it does today, over one hundred years later. There are no words accurate enough to express the insanity and the insatiability of the war's great maw for death and destruction.

Early efforts to capture in language its catastrophic effects failed as the unleashed and unparalleled violence mocked those who bravely shouted, "I'll be home for Christmas!" The bitter irony of the "short war illusion" spawned widespread disillusionment, but later terminology proved no more adequate to the task. As the enormity of the savage bloodbath took conscious hold, some took to describing calling it "The Great War"—something it surely was not. Finally, as the industrialization killed millions amidst scenes of untold carnage, came the hopeful yet hopeless appellation, "The War to End All Wars."

As people commemorate the war that few wanted or imagined, we still struggle with inadequate descriptors. "The First World War," pointing as much to the second as to itself, fails to reach the depth of four years of slaughter and insanity. The preeminent British historian of the war B. H. Liddell Hart called it "The Real War" when he first published his account in 1930. The Harvard academic J. K. Galbraith used the term "The Great Ungluing" to describe the war's brutality as well as its profound transformative effects. Perhaps, "The Suicide of European Civilization" is the best

way to try to access the war's pathology, and its voracious appetite for death and nihilistic destruction which turned Europe into a charnel house.

By August 1914, the belligerents of the Triple Entente and Central Powers quickly mobilized what eventually would become millions of combatants. By the time it ended in 1918, nations and empires had suffered staggering losses. Germany lost 2 million dead, and Austria–Hungary some 1.5 million. The British Empire recorded 1 million dead, while 1.7 million paid the ultimate price in defense of France. The Italians contributed 460,000 to this grim total, and the Russians 1.7 million before they signed a separate peace with Germany at Brest–Litovsk in March 1918.[1] Other countries suffered as well.

In August 1914, my father Leonhard Rempe, then 21 years old, heard Kaiser Wilhelm II declare from the balcony of his Schloss in Berlin that he "recognized parties no more; I recognize only Germans" and that confronted by the enemy a united Germany would defeat the invaders. On hearing this, he could only have felt the patriotic need to defend the Fatherland. My father could no more know of the complex of long- and short-range causes that led to the Kaiser's declaration than could the average GI, many years later, know that he was not actually fighting in Vietnam to contain the spread of international, monolithic communism. For all my father knew, it was imperative for him to join the colors in defending German Kultur against a Russian invasion.

However, if he could not know all of its causes, my father would know some of its effects if only by living through them. The collapse of the German, Austro-Hungarian, Russian and Ottoman empires, the Bolshevik seizure of power in Russia, the emergence of the United States as a great power, the Great Depression, occurring ten years after the signing of the Versailles Treaty, and the Second World War, clearly a toxic product of the first, are but a few of its more important consequences.

The volume of literature, as one would expect, on the war itself as well as on its causes and consequences, is simply enormous. This book does not seek to cover the latter, rather it is the personal story of a man who decided to serve the Fatherland. The voice of the individual gains immense value and importance when contrasted with the war's impersonal, grinding, mass-machinery of death. Against the commitment of the belligerent powers to engage in total apocalyptic war, we seek to hear the voices of those who lived through the insanity. Seemingly, an individual's experiences and perspectives might serve to inject a human element into that which was all too inhuman and barbaric.

This book is about my father, one of millions of combatants who fought for his country. While the personal perspective is invaluable and insightful, my father's military career is also interesting because it was somewhat unique. He joined the war in August 1914 as a cavalry member of the West Prussian Field Artillery Regiment No. 35 (Westpreußisches Feldartillerie-Regiment Nr. 35), and served in that capacity on the Eastern Front against the Russians until November 1916. Although he was not the only one to exchange the

brutalities of the Eastern Front for the "glamour" of the skies over Western Europe, or to trade the cavalry, a traditional form of warfare, for the new technology of air power (one thinks immediately of Baron Manfred von Richthofen), my father's career as a reconnaissance pilot on the Western Front in the last two years of the war provides yet another dimension to his wartime experiences. Following the Armistice in November 1918, his service continued when he joined General Georg Maercker's Freiwilliges Landesjägerkorps (Freikorps) to defend the newly formed Weimar Republic against the perceived threat of a Bolshevik takeover.

The tripartite organization of this book logically follows Leonhard's military career. Fortunately for posterity, my father saved quantities of historical materials that provide evidence for all three phases of his military service. These primary sources range from maps and battle plans for engagements on the Eastern Front to reconnaissance photos and barograph (altimeter) readings in flights over the Western Front. He also left a photo album of the war, which depicts his life on the Eastern Front as a cavalry officer, and images of his wartime experiences flying reconnaissance missions over France. Finally, in 1956, the last year of his life, my father wrote a memoir which described his life up to 1914, his experiences in the war, the immediate postwar period, and the years after 1923 when he left Germany to begin a new life in the United States.

In addition to the 1956 memoir, in 1930, seven years after his arrival in the United States, my father wrote a brief account of his military career during the war. What makes this memoir material of such interest is the relationship of the two documents to each other (the 1930 memoir was written in German while the 1956 memoir was written in English), as well as the relationship of both memoirs to the historical record of archival materials. In other words, what is the relationship of memory to history? Should one be surprised that the 1956 memoir looks back on the war years with a more positive light than the 1930 document, or that the historical record itself might warrant?

At times, the war material he saved contradicts the two memoirs he wrote later in life, and it provides a corrective to those documents. The first three chapters uses his primary source materials to provide insight into what actually happened in the three phases of his military career, while a fourth chapter presents that portion of his 1956 memoir dealing with his wartime experiences. The memoir reveals not only his talents as a writer in his adopted second language, but how he looked back upon the war then some 45 years in his past. A final brief chapter covers his life in America, and an Editor's epilogue explores the relationship of memory to history.

My contribution has been to provide a context using both Leonhard's primary source evidence as well as a range of secondary sources to document his wartime career. Although scholars may find much of interest in some of the primary sources, this short work does not pretend to be a work of professional scholarship; instead, it is meant for a general audience interested in the experiences of a German officer in the First World War and its immediate aftermath. Besides the text, I have included many of the photographs my father preserved in his war photo album.

Like so many veterans of so many wars, my father did not wish to speak of his service. When pressed, he admitted that he would never be able to suppress the cries and screams of the dying, nor scour the smell of death from his nostrils. He told me of the ear-splitting thunder of large artillery barrages, how the sky was illuminated by flares, and how the shells made an unforgettable sound when they crashed into the surrounding forest. He recalled hundreds of Russian corpses hanging on German defensive wires, how the enemy often left the battlefield without burying their dead, and the agonizing cries of the wounded and dying young German soldiers on a troop train as it slowly made its way back to Berlin.

In a talk he gave before a West Bend, Wisconsin, meeting of American Legion members in 1935, 12 years after his arrival in the United States, my father said: "I lived four long years in hell. I will not tell you anything about my experiences in the war other than to say that time will not ever erase these horrible years from my memory. After the war it was hard for me to find the way back to normal life."[2] None of the belligerents imagined the war's destructive power and its impact on future events. Indeed, the effects of the 1914–18 war manifest themselves in our own time.

Few among the political and military leaders, common soldiers, and innocent civilians had any foretaste of the mindless slaughter and complete destruction that would define this ghastly and futile war. One of the few may have been the Chief of the German General Staff, Helmuth von Moltke. On July 28, 1914, he wrote to Chancellor Theobald von Bethmann-Hollweg to urge a rapid initiation of war plans in the hope of a quick victory, as he thought a long war would be sustained and brutal with the nations of Europe tearing themselves apart and "destroying civilization in almost all of Europe for decades to come."[3]

Chapter 1

On the Eastern Front, 1914-1916

In an unfinished memoir written in German in 1930, seven years after he arrived in the United States, my father wrote: "the war is long over, years ago, and yet the memories of those great days remain fresh and unforgotten. Moreover I am thankful to have lived through that terrible struggle of nations."[1]

He recollected that, "the summer days of 1914 are clear in my mind. At that time I was in a peaceful little town with a long history in the Harz Mountains where I was studying to become a businessman at an iron works." He felt "the failed efforts of the Kaiser to preserve peace led to mobilization and unavoidable war" and he concluded that in resisting the invading Russians, "I had fought honorably and for high ideals."[2] Included in the papers he preserved is a letter which states:

> The bearer of this letter, Herr Leonhard Rempe of Alhausen, trained in my iron and household products shop from May 1, 1912 until today. I am pleased to report that he is a truthful, industrious and principled young man, who always strove to learn and to develop familiarity with the business. He performed his duties to my complete satisfaction. Herr Rempe leaves this position by choice, in order to serve the Fatherland. My best wishes go with him.

> Signed: Herr Hottenrott
> Goslar
> August 5, 1914[3]

My father's records show on that very day, August 5, he failed an initial physical at Goslar Military Hospital. However, five days later, at the military hospital in Paderborn, the chief medical officer pronounced him fit for military service with a height of 5ft 7in. and a weight of 132 pounds.[4]

In his 1930 memoir, he recounts how he "went back and forth across the country from barracks to barracks until I managed to find a spot with the *82nd Field Artillery* in Osterode with the East Prussians."[5] This unit was transferred to Perleberg due to the earlier than expected mobilization of Russian forces. Perleberg, in the northwestern part of Brandenburg state, had a long history of troops being stationed there. In his 1930 memoir, he states: "Perleberg is where I became a soldier, heart and soul. I was so proud of my uniform, the carbine, the saber, the pistols, boots and spurs, the strict service, military exercises and riding."[6]

He described a typical day while in training at Perleberg:

05:30—Reveille
07:30—Formation
07:45—08:45 Lecture

09:00—10:00 Infantry exercises
10:00—11:00 Sentry duty
11:00—12:00 Class
13:30—15:00 Weapons training
15:00—16:00 Housekeeping
16:45—17:15 Lecture

After his training at Perleberg, my father returned to Osterode to await further orders. He then learned of his transfer to the *West Prussian Field Artillery Regiment No. 35* (*Westpreußisches Feldartillerie-Regiment Nr. 35*). However, his first order came in the form of leave excusing him from immediate front-line war service in 1914:

> The bearer of this pass is to report to the responsible district commander for deployment to his unit on a yet to be determined date, carrying at a minimum a coat, boots, and shirt. Upon turning in this pass, deployment to the unit will follow immediately. Failure to report will be punished by military law.[7]

By mid-March 1915, my father was stationed at the military barracks in Deutsch-Eylau, now the Polish City of Ilawa, in the northeastern part of that country. In being attached to the *West Prussian Field Artillery Regiment No. 35*, my father joined a regiment that already had a distinguished service record. Originally formed February 1, 1890, the regiment was part of the *XX Army Corps' 41st Infantry Division*, attached to the *2nd Cavalry Division*.

In 1914, the staff of a field artillery regiment consisted of six officers (commander, adjutant, orderly officer, regimental medical officer, regimental veterinary officer, and train transport commander), 16 NCOs and other ranks, 20 horses, and one baggage wagon. The field artillery consisted of 7.7cm field guns and a 10.5cm light field howitzer.[8] *The West Prussian Field Artillery Regiment No. 35* also fought with a horse artillery detachment of three batteries of four guns each.[9]

As the war began, the *West Prussian Field Artillery Regiment No. 35* had engaged in combat at the Somme, Arras, Lille and other places on the Western Front before being sent in November to fight the invading Russian forces. In April 1915, three infantry and three cavalry divisions moved into the Russian province of Courland (Kurland, now part of modern-day Latvia) and threatened Russian rail lines from Warsaw to St Petersburg. German forces were in Courland because General Erich Ludendorff, the hero of the battle of Tannenberg (August 26–30, 1914), received orders to relieve pressure on German troops in Galicia by drawing Russian reserves north. Ludendorff complied by "launching a strong cavalry force into Courland in mid-April" as part of the newly formed *Army of the Niemen* (Njemen-Armee).[10]

On May 26, General Otto von Below, regarded as one of the best commanders, and head of the Eighth Army which defeated the Russians at the second battle of the Masurian Lakes (February 7–22, 1915), was transferred to the new *Army of the Niemen*. That May, *West Prussian Field Artillery Regiment No. 35* was with the *2nd Cavalry Division* fighting to push Russian forces further east with a goal of securing a line from Kovno (Kaunas, Lithuania) to Riga.[11]

A May, 1915, article in *The New York Times* by Walter Ives, identified as a former lieutenant in the Royal Prussian 13th Dragoons, reported of "the unexpected and sudden advance of German troops into the heart of the Russian province of Courland."

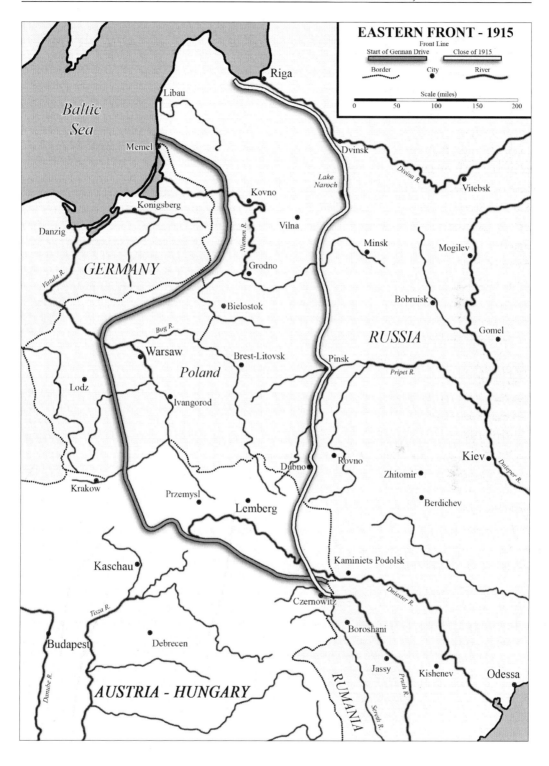

EASTERN FRONT - 1915

He wrote that the Russians were severely mistaken if they saw this advance as just an example of German adventurism; "lust for adventure," Ives wrote, "has never had any part in the plans of operation carried out by the German General Staff." Instead, Ives argued, the Germans had either a strategic goal to conquer the northwestern part of Courland "as far as a line extending from Wileny, to Schawll, Mitau and Riga" or an economic goal, namely, "a thrust against the Russian bread line from Dunaburg to Wilna and Warsaw." The author continued his article by detailing the great difficulties the Germans would face in pursuing either course of action.[12]

Before joining the Army of the Niemen in August 1915, my father had been part of a Cavalry division. He saw action with III Cavalry Corps under Oberleutnant Schaefer in the spring of 1915 near the village of Wachefka (Warszeaka). In his 1930 memoir, my father wrote about how he and 40 others, along with 40 horses, were loaded on a train to Mlawa near the Russian border. After a two-day advance, partly by truck and partly by horseback, they reached the small town of Drobin, which he characterized as being little more than a crossroads to the North Pole:

> Upon arrival, Major Stief divided us among the various batteries which held the surrounding villages. We were about 10km [6 miles] from the front lines.

> It was hard duty. Every second day we took positions, by night, 1,000m [1,100 yards] from the Russian lines and at dawn quietly pulled back 4,000m [4,400 yards] and then returned to our daytime positions. This was to deceive the Russians as to our strength. There was little shooting on either side.

> On April 5, 1915 I saw my first action when the Russians pummeled our position with heavy artillery fire. At the beginning of May, I was transferred to a newly formed flak unit under Lieutenant Schulz. We had set up a weapon on a hill and tried to shoot down enemy pilots from there. Unfortunately, we rarely got to do this. We lived in self-made shelters, well camouflaged against planes, and led, all things considered, a pleasant life.

> At the end of May, I had a horse accident, hurt my knee and ended up in the hospital in Drobin . . . I stayed there two days and then was taken by car to Plock [Podolszyce, on the River Vistula] and from there via steam-ship to Thorn [Torun]. Eight days later, and healthy, I reported to the replacement troop at Deutsch-Eylau and was given leave to see my widowed mother in Alhausen from June 15. On June 30, the last day of my leave and my 22nd birthday, I was promoted to corporal, had easy duty and rode into Remont. Later, I was only too happy to acquire a new horse and after numerous wrong turns and wonderful quarters in beautiful surroundings I reached the 2nd Cavalry Division and my old friends of the West Prussian Field Artillery No. 35 in Courland.[13]

By July, General Otto von Below, Commander of the *Army of the Niemen* on the northern side of the German front line, initiated an offensive that thundered "across the hot summer landscape like a tornado."[14]

Trench warfare soon gave way to long-imagined mobile tactics in which cavalry units attacked poorly constructed Russian lines around Schaulen (Šiauliai) in modern Lithuania. Three cavalry divisions, supported by horse artillery units incorporated within the Army of the Niemen "swept like a whirlwind that shook the leaves from the trees."[15]

My father arrived on this front at the moment the Russians mounted a strong counterattack at Kupischki (Kupiškis, Lithuania). After repulsing this attack, the Army of the Niemen was split up with the right, or southerly wing, moving against Kovno while the left, or northerly wing, was to attack and capture Mitau (Jelgava, Latvia); the latter fell in August.[16]

In his 1930 memoir, my father recorded that he had become a telephone man and that it felt good to be doing important work. He wrote: "We advanced into Kurland and fought many skirmishes which were tiring on both rider and steed." He mentioned that "the Eastern most action we saw was around Dubena on the Dubna River in eastern Latvia." Unfortunately, my father provided little detail about the skirmish at Postwai in which he was involved (see the Appendix) or about the fact he lived in the local pastor's house for eight days. His 1930 memoir does, however, provide a lengthy and vivid description of heavy fighting in front of Dünaburg (Daugavpils, Latvia) in mid-October. Dünaburg was located on the banks of the River Daugava 120km (75 miles) from Latvia's border with Russia while Riga, its capital, was 230km (140 miles) to the northwest. He wrote:

We had lain quiet peaceably across from the Russians for weeks. No skirmishes in our section. Our cavalry division had made themselves comfortable, i.e. had dug in about 800–1,000 meters [870–1,090 yards] from the enemy. We in the artillery were further back and dying to shoot. Then I suddenly got word of active construction work among the Russians.

We had the Russian elite, Siberian sharpshooters, in front of us.

Very soon came new reports of active movement on the Russian side with reinforcements arriving daily; runners and field messages intercepted by our forward units confirmed this. High alert was declared and everybody was on guard. The enemy had placed mines and spent the nights laying barbed wire. We learned the night and the hour when and where the enemy would attack us and the game would start.

To my delight, I was assigned as an observer for our artillery to the front trench with orders to direct our batteries' fire from there; here I would see the war very near at hand. As darkness fell, I reported to my section leader, established the connection with our batteries, and waited with my trench binoculars for whatever might come. Everything down to the tiniest detail had been discussed, and every man knew his orders. About 1,200 meters [1,300 yards] ahead lay a large forest with a swampy area in front. Russian trenches were clearly visible and from there the Russians wanted to push us out of our drier positions.

The moon cast its pale light eerily onto the earth and all looked quite peaceful. Our rider stood on the breastworks ready for action. We had plenty of machine guns and didn't lack for hand grenades or ammunition. We were ready to receive the Russians as I again tested the telephone connection with our batteries and found them to be in good order. The hours crept by very slowly and then, suddenly, the stillness ended as chh-chh-chh-boom the 10.5's howitzer shells flew over our heads and soon hundreds and thousands of shots from their light and heavy artillery were coming from the Russian positions. One could see very clearly the movement on the enemy's side; it is almost daylight so bright now shines the moon.

Thick masses of men seem to emerge from out of the woods as fire balls and sky rockets fly into the air, one shell exploding not far from me—have a cigarette—stay calm. The commander comes over to me as flares burst around us and numerous enemy batteries attack under deadly cover of fire. The Russians are cutting their wire. "Call it in," says my Commander; "On your order," I reply. I take my phone and soon four shots leave shrapnel just over the enemy trenches, followed by our shells smashing into the forest destroying the trees.

The Russians could be seen running back and forth providing plentiful targets. They appear bewildered and seem to have called off their attack. But then from the forest come new troops in a close-formed mass, senseless men charging shoulder to shoulder—the Russian steamroller. The poor fellows, frantic fire greets them as our machine guns start to hammer away tack, tack, tack, tack. Hell seems to have opened up and above it all the strange "Ur-rah" cries of the Russian soldiers.

Deadly courageous they come and die for their little mother Russia driven by their officers. They want to break ranks and turn back but cannot do it. Their attack lasts about thirty minutes and their dead bodies pile up on the wire. Those who make it over are quickly killed by our men. Now the rest break up in hasty flight: the attack has been repelled and all is calm as before.

There is no thought of sleep, and I wander through our trenches. We did not take great losses. A dark cloud now shrouds the moon and deserters creep into our trenches with fear and shock on their faces. Finally, night passes and the early morning light reveals a shocking picture. Our forward posts find the Russian positions abandoned. We take care of our horses, bury the dead and pursue the enemy.[17]

My father was awarded the Iron Cross Second Class on October 17, 1915 for his action that night. His 1956 memoir provides further details of his bravery under fire. Among his papers he kept several maps of the changing locations of fighting on the Eastern Front. On these maps he underlined various sites of combat including Postwai, Kupischki, Schawll (Schaulen, now Šiauliai, Lithuania), Dünaburg, and later, in 1916, Lake Naroch (Naratsch-See), Baranowitschi (Baranovichi, western Belarus) and Kovel.[18]

A letter, previously quoted, dated September 26, 1921, by the District Commander at Paderborn, Konig, certifies that *Leutnant der Reserve* (Reserve Lieutenant) Leonhard Rempe performed "active military service" at Kupischki, Dünaburg, and in battles between lakes Boginskoje and Driswiaty. The letter also confirms Leonhard's presence at the battle of Lake Naroch and Lake Driswiaty.[19]

While my father was undoubtedly proud of his Iron Cross, he also kept with his papers a certificate which states, "Leonhard Rempe was deloused today: His clothes and possessions were disinfected," signed by the garrison doctor at Kovno, and dated October 20, 1915. Within a week, he experienced the glory and the reality of war.[20]

Shortly before his delousing at Kovno, and perhaps the reason for it, was an order of October 18, 1915, to report immediately to the Field Artillery Firing School in Jüterbog, East Prussia.[21] In both the 1930 and 1956 memoirs, my father writes about his joy at being away from the front: "I was the happiest man in Jüterbog, weapons school was easy duty. I felt human again; there were good comrades and upstanding officers there—Captain Weste and General Gluck. I did well on the exams and got fourteen days leave to visit my widowed mother in Alhausen—happy times they were."[22]

Leonhard continues the narrative of events in his 1930 memoir: "Left Alhausen and back to the front by train via Vilna [Vilnius, Lithuania] and then by truck to Brzezany [Berezhany, Ukraine]. Received a warm welcome and from then on ate with the officers."[23] On December 3, he was promoted to Vizewachtmeister (Vice Watch Master) although there was little aggressive action from either Russian or German armies as each side had moved into winter quarters. He describes celebrating Christmas 1915 by drinking champagne with comrades. On January, 14, 1916, he proudly notes that "thanks to the direct order of the cabinet, I was appointed *Leutnant der Reserve* [Reserve Lieutenant]" and that "Claussen informed me by telephone on January 18."[24] The historian John H. Morrow Jr reminds us that "the German Army had trained its reserve units so well that it incorporated them into its front-line forces, unlike other armies."[25]

As the harsh winter was slowly releasing its iron grip on Russia, my father obtained military leave, dated March 12,1916, for travel to Vilna, which the Germans had captured the previous September. This leave was cut short as the Russians launched an attack on March 18 with the object of recapturing Vilna. One reason for this Russian attack was continued French pressure on the Russians to draw German troops from the Western Front; indeed, Tsar Nicholas II himself acceded to this French request and selected Lake Naroch (Naratsch-See) in Belarus because his soldiers outnumbered the Germans by between 180,000 and 300,000.[26]

In his book *The Eastern Front 1914–1917*, Norman Stone asserts that "Lake Naroch was one of the decisive battles of World War One as it condemned most of the Russians to passivity."[27] Stone concludes that the ultimate Russian defeat at Lake Naroch by the end of March led to a certain fatalism, given that Russian forces had superior numbers in both men and ammunition. John Keegan, in his book *The First World War*, agrees with Stone's assessment: "Russian forces enjoyed a large superiority in men, weapons and shells, considerably more than assembled by the Germans for the Gorlice-Tarnow break-through in 1915."[28] But, as Stone points out, superiority in men and munitions failed to overcome poor Russian planning and tactics, bad communications, and incompetent leadership characterized by rivalries among commanders.[29]

March would have been one of the worst months to mount an offensive as the uncertainties of Russian spring weather made combat extremely difficult. Stone writes that "alternating freezes and thaws made roads either ice rinks or a thick morass."[30] Professor Holger Herwig, in his book *The First World War: Germany and Austria–Hungary 1914–1918*, agrees with this assessment and writes that "Lake Naroch was covered with almost a foot of water and slush."[31] Additionally, the Russian positions were hardly combat ready while German intelligence had known of the Russian attack two weeks before it happened.[32]

My father wrote that this battle gave him an opportunity to put into practice what he had learned at the Jüterbog artillery school.[33] Professor Herwig notes that the German artillery under the command of Lieutenant-Colonel Georg Bruchmüller, considered a founder of modern artillery use with his "creeping barrage," "surprised the Russians at Lake Naroch with a hurricane-like barrage that pitted accurate artillery fire against previously identified targets." Herwig writes "of the highly centralized firing command that instructed each battery throughout the barrage."[34] With this fierce battle won by early April, German forces recaptured all the territory they had once held. The Russian Army sustained losses of about 100,000 men in addition to the c.12,000 who had died from severe frostbite. In contrast, the Germans lost about 20,000 men and claimed that they had removed at least 5,000 Russian corpses from the barbed wire.[35] The Russian defeat at the battle of Lake Naroch caused "a general unwillingness among the senior commanders to risk their reputations further." About the only Russian general willing to do so was Alexei Brusilov.[36]

It was after the battle of Lake Naroch, which lasted from March 18 to March 26, 1916, that on June 4 the brilliant Brusilov launched his massive offensive south of the Pripet Marshes in the area of the Ukraine around Lemberg (Lviv), Lutsk, and Kowel (Kovel). In what Professor G. A. Tunstall termed the Triple Entente's greatest victory and, correspondingly, the worst crisis for Austria–Hungary, three of four of Brusilov's attacking armies were able to reverse the losses of the great Russian retreat of 1915. Professor Keegan notes that Austro-Hungarian losses in the campaign amounted to 600,000 killed with

400,000 taken prisoner along with German losses of around 350,000.[37] In The First World War: Germany and Austria–Hungary 1914–1918, Herwig states that it was only General Felix von Bothmer's *Sudarmee* (South Army) that temporarily held the line before retreating to a line marked by Brody–Lemberg and Kowel. He also took note that, as a result of General Alexander von Linsingen's counterattack, General Bothmer's position was finally stabilized on the River Styr. Because of this German effort to aid Austro-Hungarian forces, Herwig agrees with those historians who see the Brusilov offensive as the virtual end of Austrian–Hungarian power and its complete dependence upon German military might.[38]

My father notes in his 1930 memoir that by the end of June 1916 the West Prussian Field Artillery Regiment No. 35 had been transferred to Baranovichi. "I am made an ordinance officer on the General Staff and go on leave at Derewnia [Derevnya, Ukraine]. Scarcely home, I am ordered back by telegraph."[39] He writes: "at Moldschatz, I find my unit in the toughest action yet. We suffered bad losses. Captain Schaefer dead, Greves badly wounded. We held off all attacks but had a difficult time here in the Eastern Reich."[40]

At this time, my father was an artillery liaison officer attached to an Austro-Hungarian k.u.k. (kaiserlich und königlich, Imperial and Royal) regiment, most likely the Hungarian 38th Honvéd Regiment, in support of the German 48th Reserve Division of the *Sudarmee* (South Army) near the town of Brzezany (Berezhany, Ukraine). Although his 1956 memoir minimizes his combat as an artillery liaison officer, he saw action in Kowel (Kovel) and later on the River Styr.[41] From mid-August, he was in the 2nd Cavalry Division as part of Army Group Eben, which fought along with the k.u.k. Second Army.[42] He continued with the 2nd Cavalry Division in the k.u.k. XVIII Korps (Imperial and Royal XVIII Corps) as part of the Horse Artillery Battalion of the West Prussian Field Artillery Regiment No. 35. On July 28 he was involved in trench fighting west of Brody in Western Ukraine, and he took part in continued, bitter trench fighting between Narajowka and Zlota-Lipka.

In mid-1916, the Leib-Husaren-Brigade, made up of the 1st and 2nd Leib-Husaren regiments, had become part of the 2nd Cavalry Division. The fact that Oberleutnant Friedrich Karl Prinz von Preussen was a member of 1st Leib-Husaren-Regiment would later have momentous consequences for my father.

In September, still fighting with the South Army, my father was involved in conflict at Brzezany, and later with the Austro-Hungarian k.u.k. Second Army in trench fighting in Eastern Galicia. However as a result of military leave, signed on November 8, he was given permission to visit his mother in Alhausen from November 10 to 30. It was here, in Alhausen, that a telegram reached him on November 18 stating that he should "come to Breslau immediately."[43]

Leonhard R. Rempe, pictured in August 1914.

A cannon and crew of the 1st Battery, *West Prussian
Field Artillery Regiment No. 35* in Courland.

A gun and crew of the 1st Battery, *West Prussian Field Artillery Regiment No. 35.*

A field kitchen, *West Prussian Field Artillery Regiment No. 35.*

Dr. Richter, the regimental medical officer of *West Prussian Field Artillery Regiment No. 35.*

Wachtmeister Draeger of *West Prussian Field Artillery Regiment No. 35.*

A Maxim gun (left) and an MG08 (right) and their crews.

Railway Station at Vilna, Russia (Lithuania). Note: German flag flying atop the station.

The grim task of burial detail.

Cavalry unit casualties included horses as well as men.

A destroyed bridge in Vilna, Russia (Lithuania) in 1915.

Lake Driswiaty, the scene of fighting (part of the larger Lake Naroch battle)
in which Leonhard Rempe participated.

Top left: *Leutnant der Reserve* Rempe exiting a bunker on the Eastern Front.
Top right: From left to right, *Kameraden* Becker, Worm, and Ritgen on the Eastern Front.
Worm and Ritgen display the *EKII* (Iron Cross Second Class) ribbon on their uniforms.

Officers celebrate Christmas 1915. Leonhard Rempe is on the far right.

Rempe (left) during his final exam at Jüterbog.

Leutnant der Reserve Rempe, on the left, during a study break in his preparations
for his final exams at Jüterbog Artillery School.

October 20, 1915, Rempe has been deloused and his clothing disinfected at Kovno.

Early pages from 1930 memoir written in German. This 1930 memoir was never completed.

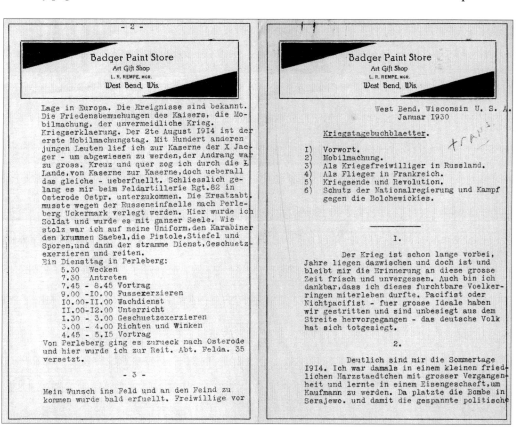

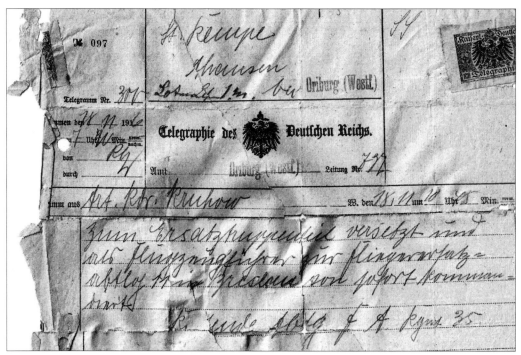

Telegram dated Nov 18, 1916 ordering Rempe to Breslau for flight training.

Military training pass from Alhausen, no destination given, via Kovno.

Colonel Georg Bruchmüller's artillery firing instructions, August 25, 1916 from Baranovichi.

Chapter 2

Over the Western Front,
1916–1918

By November 1916 my father was hardly the only one making an assessment of the situation on the Eastern Front. He believed it would take the Russians a long time to recover from their defeat at Lake Naroch; in fact, he thought the spirit of the Russian Army was virtually broken despite the success of General Brusilov's campaign. This assessment, plus a desire—according to his 1956 memoir—to seek a more glorious theater for action, led him to contemplate the possibility of leaving the Eastern Front to join the nascent German Air Force, the *Luftstreitkräfte*.[1]

Military leave to Alhausen and Paderborn, dated November 8, 1916, provided an opportunity to make a major change in Leonhard's wartime experiences.[2] On November 18 he received a telegram ordering him immediately to Breslau for transfer to Flight Replacement Unit (*Fliegerersatzabteilung—FEA*) 11 at Hundsfeld, near Breslau.[3] Upon reporting at Breslau, my father expressed to the commanding officer his desire to train as a pilot at Hundsfeld Military Flight School. In turn, the commanding officer "suggested" he train as an observer since he had a good deal of experience as an artillery officer on the Eastern Front. At this precise moment

Prince Friedrich Karl von Preussen, a nephew of the Kaiser, appeared in the office. He had served on the Eastern Front with the 1st Leib-Husaren Regiment, and he knew my father because this regiment was part of the 2nd Cavalry Division.[4]

The prince, who was my father's age, had been a member of Germany's 1912 equestrian team and had won a bronze medal in the Stockholm Olympics of that year. Now he supported my father's request to train as a pilot at Hundsfeld.[5] The latter had been the first school for pilot training and it provided an increasing number of aviators from the ranks of non-commissioned officers and enlisted men.[6] My father notes, somewhat sardonically, that the prince required only a month of pilot's training "as he had an instructor and two machines at his disposal, and it took me three months to complete the course because forty other officers and I had only one instructor and one airplane."[7]

Actually, a three-month training period was close to the norm and during his course of instruction my father flew in more than one type of aircraft. One of the documents he saved is the record book of his training period at Hundsfeld. His flight book records 85 flights between November 25, 1916 and February 17, 1917 and provides information on weather conditions including gusty winds, rain, heavy fog and frost. He gives the name of his principal flight instructor and how often he flew in the front or back cockpit of the plane.[8]

According to interrogations of captured German pilots by British intelligence officers, the German system of pilot training was quite rigorous. At Hundsfeld, where most of the students were either officers or non-commissioned officers, the trainee had instruction in map and compass reading as well as in aircraft construction and engine maintenance.[9] Their course lasted between four and six weeks, but bad weather and the lack of aircraft often meant a more extensive training period.

The course required a successful completion of three examinations after the student passed an oral exam on the aircraft, its engine and its controls. Even before the first exam, the student made 30 flights with his instructor in order to achieve his first solo flight. While the first exam consisted of making ten figure eights from 390 to 500ft (120–150m) and landing the aircraft on a prearranged spot after the fifth and tenth figure, the second and third exams became progressively more difficult. Among the requirements for the second exam were multiple landings from various heights with full fuel tanks and ballast in place of an observer. Having passed the second exam, there was an additional training period for aerial combat practice of seven or eight weeks before the final exam. Originally, the entire course was meant to take about six months, but times were shortened to about four and a half to three and a half months as the war demanded more pilots.

The final exam required five landings from different heights as well as five landings on unknown ground upon which landing signals had been placed. Other requirements were two 60-mile (100km) flights with an observer during which prearranged objects were to be photographed, an altitude test of 11,500ft (3,500m) with an observer as well as aerial combats against the instructor and observer in an "enemy" aircraft. Perhaps it is not surprising that only 50 percent of those accepted into the course actually became pilots.[10]

While my father trained with several different aircraft, including L.V.G.s, once in combat zones he flew mostly Rumpler C.IV and C.VII machines. Of the former, Peter Grosz, a leading expert on Rumpler aircraft and the son of the important Weimar Expressionist George Grosz, writes: "the Rumpler C.IV is generally considered one of the best two-seater German aircraft of World War One."[11]

Dr John Morrow, an authority on the 1914–18 air war, notes that "British aces had a healthy respect for Rumpler two-seater crews because of their superior performance above 17,000 feet."[12] In another work, Morrow contrasts the British view of air power, which generally favored fighter aircraft, with the German understanding of the value of reconnaissance aircraft: "The Germans, in contrast, sent expert crews alone and at high altitudes in superior Rumpler and DFW biplanes, formidable opponents even for highly skilled fighter pilots."[13]

Both of these machines carried a pilot and an observer and were developed for reconnaissance purposes. As the war in the West settled into static trench warfare, reconnaissance flights provided the "eyes of

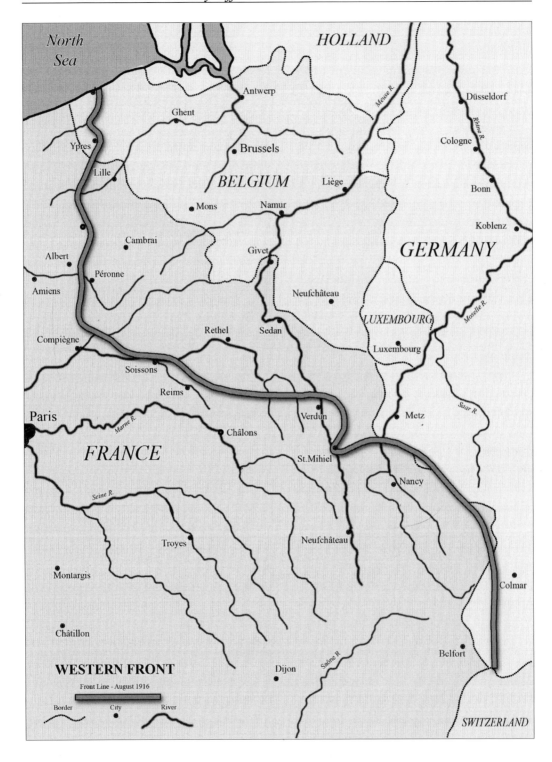

North
Sea

HOLLAND

Antwerp

Ghent

Ypres

Brussels

Lille

BELGIUM

Liège

Mons

Namur

Düsseldorf

Rhine R.

Cologne

Bonn

Koblenz

Meuse R.

Cambrai

Givet

GERMANY

Albert

Péronne

Amiens

Neufchâteau

LUXEMBOURG

Moselle R.

Compiègne

Rethel

Sedan

Luxembourg

Soissons

Reims

Paris

Marne R.

Verdun

Metz

Saar R.

Châlons

FRANCE

St.Mihiel

Seine R.

Nancy

Troyes

Neufchâteau

Montargis

Colmar

Châtillon

Belfort

WESTERN FRONT

Front Line - August 1916

Dijon

Saône R.

Border   City   River

SWITZERLAND

the army" in gathering a variety of military intelligence. The C.IV was powered by a Mercedes D.IV, a water-cooled in-line engine which developed 260hp. It could reach a speed of 107mph and a service ceiling of 21,000ft and as such it possessed not only speed but also long-range, high-altitude capability.[14] It was armed with one fixed forward-firing 7.92mm light machine gun and one 7.92mm Parabellum machine gun mounted on a swivel for the observer.[15] The C.IV had 50 and 70cm cameras on board for long-range artillery spotting and close-reconnaissance photography.[16]

The C.VII developed from the C.IV and its most significant change was the substitution of the Mercedes engine with a Maybach Mb.Iva power plant capable of 245hp. While this was less horsepower than the Mercedes, the Maybach over-compressed engine was more efficient at higher altitudes. Morrow writes: "among the observation planes in service, the Rumpler C.VII remained superlative."[17] Grosz adds that an early test of the Maybach overcompressed engine in April 1917 took the aircraft to 5,000m (16,404ft) in 24 minutes and recorded a ceiling that was later raised to 7,000m (22,965ft). As such, "the Maybach engined Rumpler C.IV and subsequent derivatives were to become the workhorses for performing high-altitude reconnaissance work deep within enemy territory."[18]

There were two basic versions of the C.VII: the standard wireless-equipped plane, and the Rubild *Reihenbild Flugzeuge* or "strip photography aircraft," which could automatically take three overlapping photographs per minute of important targets.[19] In addition to photographic intelligence, reconnaissance aircraft were increasingly equipped with wireless telegraphy in order to spot artillery fire and to communicate with artillery batteries on the ground; the observer was responsible for sending and receiving the wireless messages, which greatly helped the accuracy of artillery fire.[20] Also, as another way to communicate messages, aviators used flare signals in various colors. For example, my father's papers preserve a signaling code, including the signal of one red star cartridge meaning "I have to make an emergency landing."[21] Flash signals could also direct fire for ground batteries. However, as Ernest von Hoeppner, Commanding General of the Air Force from October 1916, explained, "flash signals to the ground batteries caused much inconvenience in that it invited fire in return."[22]

Capable of flying at over 20,000ft at 100mph, the C.VII was out of reach of most antiaircraft fire as well as most single-seat fighter aircraft. Just as the Western Front gained more attention than the fighting on the Eastern Front, so single-seat fighter pursuit planes have gained more glory than reconnaissance aircraft and their pilots. While the more glamorous actions were associated with the members of the *Jagdstaffeln* (fighter squadrons, abbreviated to *Jasta*)—hunter groups—the German Army used its air arm primarily for recon-naissance. The *Jasta* units—such as those commanded by Oswald Boelcke, Manfred von Richthofen, and other German fighter aces—certainly received more attention, but as late as August 1918, 50 percent of German aircraft were designated for reconnaissance activity while 42 percent were described as pursuit planes and 8 percent used for bombing.[23]

Ari Unikoski describes the many challenges of reconnaissance flying:

> Reconnaissance missions were dangerous. They were usually carried out by a crew of two. The pilot was required to fly straight and level to allow the observer to take a series of overlapping photographs . . . Navigation on such flights was often a problem and should a problem develop the aircraft was far away from friendly territory . . . the bravery of the airmen in fulfilling this dangerous and unglamorous work is seldom remarked.[24]

"True, it was impossible for us to protect our observation planes against attack by enemy fliers when they were too far behind the hostile front, the enemy was too great for that," admitted General von Hoeppner in his book *Germany's War in the Air: The Development and Operations of German Military Aviation in the World War.* "Our planes invariably carried home the traces of the battles in which they had fought."[25] In an earlier part of his study, von Hoeppner waxed eloquent about German reconnaissance squadrons:

> These men, for the most part young, were enthused with an ardor as unique as their mission was special in nature. When you fly at altitudes where the lungs need the assistance of oxygen, when you see above you and around you tanks filled with a highly flammable substance, when you feel yourself carried along amid bursting shells by a motor of more than a hundred horse power with its roar deadening the human voice, you must agree that pilot and observer need a

peculiar type of courage in handling the stick, machine gun, bomb release or wireless key. As his encouragement in combat the aviator does not have the example of his leader who goes before him or the shouts of comrades by his side. All he has to sustain him is the unswerving devotion to duty.[26]

Because reconnaissance flights were of great military importance, pilots were instructed to avoid aerial combat. A captured German document from May 18, 1918 stipulates: "when the enemy is in great numerical superiority the lines should be reached by banking, zig-zag flying, spinning and diving."[27] The same captured document spells out what the trained observers were looking for, and it required the observer immediately upon landing to report enemy troop concentrations, railways, munitions dumps, roads and trenches as well as any changes in trench lines. Those engaged in photographic reconnaissance were also to report on the number of photographs taken and the area photographed as well as enemy aircraft activity and the effectiveness of anti-aircraft guns. Observers who flew on missions of artillery reconnaissance were to report on the number of field batteries and trench mortars as well as active antiaircraft emplacements and the activity of friendly and enemy artillery.[28] Morrow asserts that "German observers were much better trained than their allied counterparts."[29]

General von Hoeppner states: "the performance of the flyers (and observers) who reported comprehensive information daily surprised the High Command who initially were somewhat dubious about its value, but as the war continued the value of aerial reconnaissance became more apparent."[30] As an example of this new reality, von Hoeppner quotes a commander of an army, who concluded: "it is entirely due to the aerial reconnaissance that we knew about the preparations for the great Aisne-Champagne campaign battle and could make our preparations in due time . . . an inestimable service."[31]

Obviously the observer's role on reconnaissance missions was critical. *Leutnant* Graf Julius von Soden was usually my father's observer. It was most often the case that while pilots were non-commissioned officers, the observers were officers. Nevertheless, good relationships prevailed between pilot and observer, and they often bore the nicknames Emil and Franz.[32]

Although flying at very high altitudes between 15,000 and 22,000ft (4,500–6,700m) gave the pilot and his observer some protection from enemy fighter pilots and antiaircraft shells, the duty was difficult and hazardous. Rumpler reconnaissance aircraft were a challenge to fly and not suited for the novice pilot as they were known to be unstable in windy conditions. The C.IV was the aircraft most frequently flown by my father. Regarding this airplane, Peter Grosz, an expert on Rumplers, notes that "while the aircraft exceeded all types in climb speed ... turns had to be made with the greatest caution and care to maintain speed because the plane was prone to stall and go into a spin."[33] My father's flight report for September 18, 1917 provides evidence of this tendency to stall when he laconically records: "flight not successful, aircraft slipped at 5,200m [over 17,000ft] and straightened out only at 1,900m [6,233ft]."[34]

Apart from the eccentricities of the Rumpler aircraft, high-altitude reconnaissance flights posed other challenges. My father kept several barograph, or altimeter, readings from some of his flights. Some show he made extended flights at 2,500m (just over 8,000ft) and others indicate flying at 6,000m (close to 19,700ft). Although these altitudes allowed some immunity from enemy aircraft and antiaircraft flak, the price paid for this "luxury" was often very high. Flying in open cockpits, pilot and observer wore electrically heated flight suits and breathed oxygen connected to primitive oxygen-producing equipment.[35]

Morrow writes: "physical stress of high altitude flights in open cockpits, especially in winter, was devastating even on the younger pilots who were selected for their physical conditioning. Crews often died of the bends, or in spasms or in fits after landing." Nevertheless, Morrow concludes, "the receipt of the Rumplers was an event in a squadron's experience since they gave their crews a feeling of immense superiority and patriotic pride in such technological achievement."[36]

Although the Germans felt the chief value of airpower was in reconnaissance, as noted by Morrow,[37] this did not mean that German reconnaissance pilots in their high-flying machines always avoided combat. My father kept some of his flight reports dating from September 10, 1917 to January 29, 1918, and in some of them he notes combat with enemy aircraft. For example, on September 30, 1917, flying a Rumpler C.IV, with the designated task of "flight hunting" (*Jagdflug*), my father records "one combat with one Caudron G.3, no success, 10km [6 miles] behind our lines over the Reims area."[38] On another occasion, December 11, 1917, this time acting as an observer, my father noted "negative combat with a Spad." Again, on January 25, 1918, he notes: "above Renneville combat with a 240hp Spad that forced the aircraft back to the Marne." A final entry in the flight reports which he saved, dated January 29, 1918, records my father flying a Rumpler C.VII: "at end of the mission attacked by a Spad from 200m below, turned off after he got phosphorus bullets. Met a 300hp Breguet over enemy territory, 200m higher . . . did not attack, heavy but poorly aimed flak. Much flight activity on the front."[39]

But the main point of reconnaissance flying was to gather intelligence and not to engage in aerial combat. For example, on September 10, 1917 my father notes: "behind enemy lines, one Spad, we did not attack." Again, on September 22, he records: "two Spad very high, did not attack." Reconnaissance flights yielded a variety of information. On September 25,1917, for example, using a strip camera (*Reihenbild*), he notes: "350 photos of railroad Fismes–Bouleuse–Reims no combat, no flak". In another three hour flight, on October 1, 1917, my father reports: "RB [*Reihenbild*] photos of installations at Bouleuse–Romigny–Dormans–Épernay. Airfields around Bouleuse normal activity." He notes how his observer, von Soden, took 150 RB photos showing five Caudrons and one Spad at the Matougues Airfield and that there was no combat and the flak was sparse and poor; "near Mourmelon strange rockets with smoke tails in large numbers reached up to 4,500m [14,763ft]."[40]

At other times, instead of high-altitude reconnaissance, flights focused on low-level strafing of enemy trenches. For instance, on October 17, 1917, flying over the front lines of the German First and Seventh armies, my father reported "machine-gun strafing of enemy trenches at South Hohe with 200 bullets against strong but poorly aimed flak."[41] Three days after this mission, on October 21, 1917, my father received the coveted pilot's badge (*Flugzeugführerabzeichen*) as part of Flieger-Abteilung (*Artillerie*) 261 equipped for artillery spotting. The award from the Commanding General of the Air Services (*Kommandierender General der Luftstreit-kräfte*—abbreviated to *Kogenluft*) was designated F1.1 Nr. 112034 and was awarded on October 13 but given in the field on October 21.[42]

He repeated this strafing mission on December 10, 1917, but this time as an observer, reporting: "lively enemy flying activity behind their lines. Machine strafing of trenches at South Hohe with 200 bullets. No combat."[43] Morrow notes that in 1917 and 1918 German aircraft "staged increasingly aggressive strikes on ground troops."[44]

In his flying career, my father experienced more than one crash landing. Writing to him in the United States on September 19, 1938, 20 years after the war had ended, a Mr Ludwig Kaempffe reminded my father of what he had written in the Kaempffe house guestbook on May 20, 1917. In this book, he wrote how he feared a scolding since he had been forced to land his aircraft on a well-ordered turnip field and had caused serious crop damage, but how grateful he was since, instead of a scolding, he had been welcomed into their hospitable home.

Apparently my father made up for the damage by providing Herr Kaempffe with some gasoline for farm operations. On January 6, 1918, a still grateful Herr Kaempffe wrote to thank him for the fuel and then related this story from Christmas 1917 about his little daughter, Alli:

> Just before Christmas Eve, one of Alli's dear aunts told her that she had seen something out the window along Main Street. It had pure white wings, and flew by without a sound. The poor aunt was quite disappointed by Alli's quick and less-than-poetic answer, which was literally, 'Oh, was it Rempe?' Unfortunately, I did not catch my sister-in-law's face, but I'm sure she was crestfallen. Since then we have often laughed about the Christ Child disguised as pilot Rempe.[45]

Kaempffe's 1918 letter continues by describing some of the larger hunts in the area: "In the past week, over the course of two hunts, I got no less than 179 rabbits, and three more hunts are scheduled in the coming weeks." Herr Kaempffe complained that the cost of hunting had increased severely from paying eight or nine pfennig per shell to the ridiculous current price of between 28 and 32 pfennig per shell. He concluded his January 1918 letter by inviting my father to stay with him and his family as his guest.[46]

When he was not flying, *Leutnant der Reserve* Rempe enjoyed the companionship and lifestyle of other officers. For example, the officers' mess on December 15, 1917 offered oxtail soup, steak filets, potato croquettes, celery salad, and rice pudding. Even more elaborately, on Christmas Eve of that year the officers of *Flieger-Abteilung* (*Artillerie*) 261 dined on oysters, roast pork, red cabbage, potatoes, roast goose, apple compote, and rice pudding.[47]

There was also time for leisurely activities, card games and *Feste* to celebrate comradeship and to relieve the stress of wartime flying. His papers, for example, preserve several theater play bills. *Charleys Tante* was performed at Rethel on February 10, 1918 for the First Army. The *Rape of the Sabine Women* was also performed there on February 14, 1918.[48]

My father enjoyed hunting, and the documents he saved indicate several military passes to engage in hunting. One example, Hunting Permit No. 347, gives permission to hunt within the command district of Sery for a month's duration valid from March 10, 1918.[49] Unfortunately, he was unable to fully use the hunting permit, because on March 21, 1918 he became the hunted.

By March 1918, the course of the war had profoundly changed. It was clear, contrary to the Schlieffen Plan, which had called for the initial capitulation of France before seeking to defeat Imperial Russia, that the Leninist Revolution of November 1917 meant the future surrender of the newly installed Soviet regime. After protracted negotiations, the Bolsheviks signed the draconian Treaty of Brest-Litovsk on March 3, 1918, imposed by the victorious Imperial German government. Now that Russia was out of the war, the German military machine could concentrate all its forces on the Western Front. General Erich Ludendorff, First Quartermaster-General of the German General Staff, now planned to move 192 available divisions against the Allied forces in the West opposing him with 172 divisions.[50]

According to General von Hoeppner, even before the German artillery commenced its firing at 04:00 on March 21, 1918, the air force had already done a large part of its reconnaissance work.[51] Ludendorff's initial offensive, Operation Michael, began that day with a massive 4,000-gun barrage on a "fifty-mile wide front, Arras–St. Quentin–La Fère."[52] Paul Fussell notes that this attack in the area of the Somme cost the British 150,000 causalities and 90,000 prisoners of war almost immediately, while within six days of the German offensive the British suffered 300,000 casualties.[53]

My father, and his observer von Soden, began that very same day with another reconnaissance mission over Reims and Épernay. Quite suddenly, a Spad from *Groupe de Combat 12*—the famous French flying group the Storks (*Cigognes*)—came out of the sun and surprised my father and von Soden. Although one of their more famous aces, Georges Guynemer, had been shot down in November 1917, the Storks had many great French pilots including Albert Deullin and Alfred Heurtaux and as such "they epitomized French fighter aviation."[54]

My father, writing in his 1956 memoir, claimed it was Guynemer who attacked him, but this was clearly impossible. He describes how he thought the Frenchmen was the superior flyer and how he suddenly felt the searing pain of a bullet as it ripped into his cockpit, shattered the control stick and injured a finger in his left hand. He quickly lost control of his aircraft and plunged to the ground near Reims in no man's land. He and von Soden were able to make it to the German lines.[55]

His papers preserve a medical tag, dated March 21, 1918, which stated that a bullet wound to the left hand and third finger had been bandaged at 4:00 p.m. and a tetanus shot given at 8:00 p.m. Two days later, on March 23, my father was awarded the Iron Cross First Class (*EKI*).[56]

After a period of recovery and recuperation, and six days before General Ludendorff launched Operation Gneisenau —his fourth major offensive against Allied troops in France—my father received in Driburg a telegram on June 3, 1918 from Braunschweig requiring him to "return immediately."[57] In Braunschweig he received orders transferring him from *Flieger-ersatzabteilung 7* to his older unit, *Flieger-Abteilung (Artillerie) 261*. He was ordered to depart Braunschweig on June 6 at 13:15 and to arrive in Cologne on June 7 at 08:28. Once there, he was to take the next available train to the headquarters of his former unit. On the back of this order, my father wrote: "I hereby certify that I was instructed by the Commander and/or aide-de-camp to proceed to my unit via the quickest and shortest possible way."[58] His records also preserve travel pass No. 1815, issued by the military government of Namur on June 7, providing second class travel on military rail lines from Namur to Rethel via Charleville with the note that "Lt. of the Reich Rempe, (*Flieger-Abteilung 261(A)* is ordered to the Rethel Information Officer."[59] He reported to the latter one day after General Ludendorff called off another campaign, which had begun on May 27.

The Blücher-Yorck offensive, named after the Prussian generals who fought against Napoleon, also called the third battle of the Aisne, managed to come within 35 miles (56km) of Paris before the advance halted as a result of a lack of reserves and supplies as well as the unexpected resistance of newly arrived United States forces at Château-Thierry and Belleau Wood.[60]

The reality of loss was brought home to my father in deeply personal ways, as throughout the war he witnessed the deaths of many of his comrades. In his papers he kept a poignant letter from the father of one of his fellow pilots, *Oberleutnant* Caspar Kulenkampff-Post. His son lost his life on June 20, 1918, as a result of a defective propeller. His grief-stricken father, Dr of Law Hermann Kulenkampff-Post, wrote to my father on June 24:

> I just received a telegram stating that the transportation of my son has been barred until September, and that my son will be buried at the military cemetery in Rethel.

As Dr Kulenkampff-Post continued his letter, he asked for a report of his son's death, details of the burial ceremony and, if possible, a few photos. He concluded:

> My son often told me and wrote me that he enjoyed the best of his flying career in your division/squadron, and it is a comfort and relief to know that he died and will find eternal rest with you. Please allow me to express my warmest greetings and thanks to all the gentlemen who stood by him.[61]

Undoubtedly, the death of his friend affected him because a few days after the receipt of that letter, my father scribbled on the back of a note: "In case of my death please notify Ltn. Rempe," and with that note he provided his brother Karl's regiment number.[62]

My father has no flight reports from June when he returned to *Flieger- Abteilung (Artillerie) 261*. Instead, his papers preserve a copy of a hunting license issued in Sery and valid for August. On August 9, he was awarded a badge for suffering a wound during wartime—*Verwun-detenabzeichen* No. 22279— signed by *Kogenluft* Ernst von Hoeppner.[63]

On September 15, my father was given leave, signed by the cavalry captain divisional commander and bearing the stamp of Flieger-Abteilung (*Artillerie) 261*, through October 13 for travel from Driburg to Brussels, Ghent, Antwerp and Bruge. Instructions indicated not to speak of military matters for fear of spies and not to answer questions. Apparently traveling "for professional reasons," he was provided with rations of meat and bread as well as pay.[64]

By September, German defeat was all but inevitable. By this time, United States forces were arriving in France at more than 250,000 per month while there was a growing insufficiency of German troops.[65] The Allied blockade was also extremely effective in creating severe food and material shortages for the civilian population; already by January 1918 massive strikes had occurred in Germany. Now, in September, Ludendorff announced to General Paul von Hindenburg that an armistice was the only course of action if the army was to be brought home in order. Indeed, Keegan concludes, "The last disciplined act of the old Imperial Army was to march back across German frontiers with France and Belgium. Once on home territory, it dissolved itself."[66]

Ludendorff resigned October 26, to be succeeded by General Wilhelm Groener. By November 6 Groener was demanding that the new chancellor, Prince Max von Baden, declare an armistice. Three days later Max von Baden bestowed the title of chancellor on Friedrich Ebert, head of the majority socialists, the Social Democratic Party of Germany (*Sozialdemokratische Partei Deutschlands—SPD*). At noon on that day, against Ebert's wishes, another member of the SPD, Philipp Scheidemann, proclaimed Germany a republic, and by the end of the day, Ebert had reached an agreement with Wilhelm Groener that he would support the new Social Democratic government, "provided that it did not drastically reform the officer corps."[67] Two days later, on November 11, the Armistice was declared and the Kaiser was on his way to exile in the Netherlands.

There is next to nothing in my father's files that reflects this turmoil and revolutionary change. His only evidence from this dramatic period is an order dated November 13, 1918 which states: "Lt. Gadeymann and Lt. Rempe with D.F.W. aircraft are to report to *FEA [Fliegerersatzabteilung*—Flight Replacement Unit] 3 in Gotha for the purpose of demobilization."[68]

Two days later, my father received authorization for 250 gallons of gasoline in order to remove his plane from Hulster. This order, a sign of the new regime in Germany, is signed by Herr Lt. Heinrichs of the Workers and Soldiers Council of Siegburg. A receipt from Gotha, dated November 23, dryly notes: "this certifies that airplane pilot Lt. Rempe from the First Army, Flier Section 261 (A) correctly turned in the plane."[69]

Chapter 2 Photos

General der Luftstreitkräfte
Ernst von Hoeppner.

Three of Rempe's *Kameraden* (comrades):
von Heydebreik, von Goetze, and Folsche.

Hundsfeld Airfield near Breslau (now Wroclaw, Poland); Leonhard joined
Fliegerersatzabteilung 11 here in November 1916.

Flight school at Hundsfeld. *Leutnant der Reserve* Rempe is in the cockpit.

The Officers' Mess, Hundsfeld.

Frohes Fest—Christmas celebrations at Hundsfeld.

More Christmas celebrations at Hundsfeld.

From left to right: von Jagow, Romig, unknown, Kohl and Schmarger
at Hundsfeld, enjoying a game of skat.

From left to right: Schulz, Steinhauser and Kulenkampff-Post,
relaxing between flight duty.

Bottom Left: Army Flying Headquarters at Rethel, France.
Bottom Right: *Rittmeister* Manfred von Richthofen (the Red Baron), second from right.

Top Left: A wreath dropped by British airmen
to honor the memory of the German ace
Leutnant Max Immelmann.

Top Right: The note accompanying the wreath
dropped by British airmen to honor
Leutnant Immelmann.

Graf Julius von Soden, Rempe's
principal observer.

Left: Manfred von Richthofen (standing, right
foreground) shakes hands with a comrade. The
spurs on his boots are testament to his service as
a cavalry officer on the Eastern Front. The tail
of the aircraft behind him belongs to an
Albatros, a plane flown by many aces.

A Linke-Hofmann R.I, a prototype of one of the larger
German planes used to bomb enemy targets.

A reconnaissance photo of Vitry-le-François on the Marne River, about 112 miles east of Paris.

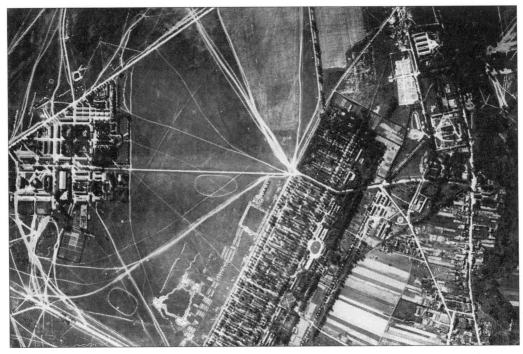

A reconnaissance photo of Mourmelon-le-Grand, France, southeast of Reims.

Looking down upon a French Voisin, a 2-seat single-engine biplane, with the
trench systems of the Western Front below.

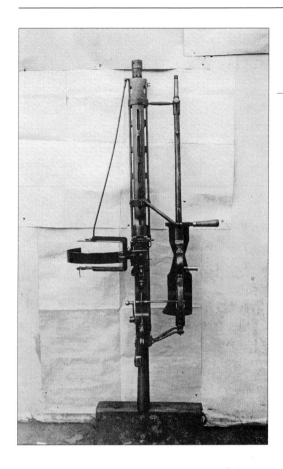

The machine gun used by Graf Julius von Soden, Leonhard Rempe's observer.

Medical tag showing Rempe had a wound bandaged March 21, 1918 at 4 and a tetanus shot at 8.

A Rumpler C.IV of the type flown by Leonhard Rempe over the Western Front.

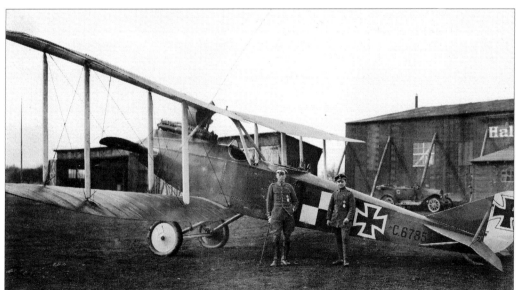

Leonhard Rempe (right) with a bandaged left hand. He was wounded during a flight on March 21, 1918.

Caspar Liborius Kulenkampff-Post, who was killed in action on June 20, 1918.

"Mein bruch"—the result of one of Rempe's crashes during his flying service.

A military funeral, with guard of honor.

The wreckage of Rempe's Rumpler C.IV near Reims; note the lightning bolt insignia on the starboard wing upper surface.

The Ninth Army field hospital, where Leonhard Rempe recuperated from his wounds.

From left to right, front row: Rempe, unknown, Soden, Schültz, Beroldingen, Steinhauser, Exss, Predohl, Predohl, unknown; back row: unknown, Mühlenbruch, Kulenkampff-Post, unknown, Redern, Heldbek, and Uir.

This picture was probably taken when the commanding officer of *Flieger-Abteilung (Artillerie) 261* left the unit. From left to right, front row: Rempe, Soden, Schülz, Beroldingen, Steinhauser, Predohl, Predohl, Fleming; back row: unknown, Exss, Redern, Mühlenbruch, unknown, Kulenkampff-Post. The remaining three are unknown.

A page from Rempe's flight training log.

Lfd. Nr.	Da-tum	Tages-zeit	Wetter	Lehrer	Schulflüge vorn	hinten	Allein-flüge	Sonstiger Dienst
47.	*Januar* 12	vorm. nachm.	gut Frost "	Schlossarek	4	–		Flugzeugdienst Unterricht
48	13	vorm. nachm.	" "	Schlossarek	4	–		Flugdienst "
49	14	vorm. nachm.	sehr gut Frost "					Flugdienst "
50	15	vorm. nachm.	Schneegestöber "	Schlossarek	10	–		Unterricht dienstfrei

The new commanding officer of *Flieger-Abteilung (Artillerie) 261*,
Cranz (fourth from left in the front row) with men of the unit.

Rempe's name on officer list, March 7, 1917.

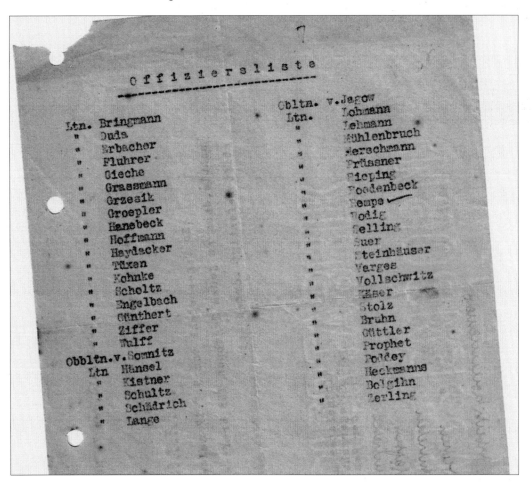

Fliegerabteilung. (A) 261

Datum: 22. 9. 1917.

Flughafen: Eoly

1. Karte: 1 : 300000

2. Flugzeug: Rumpler C 4

Führer: Lt. Rempe

Beobachter: Lt. Graf v. Soden

3. Flugzeit: 5 Uhr 30 - 6 Uhr 30 nachm.

4. Witterung und Sicht: Starker Dunst gut

5. Flugweg: Eoly - Reims - Gruppe Prosnes - Eoly.

6. Flugergebnisse (in der Flugrichtung aufgezählt):

Jagdflug.

2 Spads in grosser Höhe griffen nicht an.

Graben bei Gruppe Prosnes mit M. G.(200 Schuss)beschossen.

Schwaches Flakfeuer.

7. Kampftätigkeit:

8. Besondere Ereignisse:

Unterschrift:

Graf v. Soden Lt.

Druck von Carl Ebus, Frankfurt a. M.

An example of reconnaissance flight report dated September 22, 1917.

A document showing altimeter readings from one of Rempe's flights.

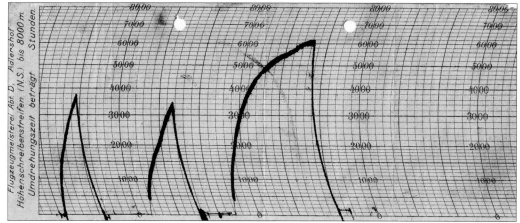

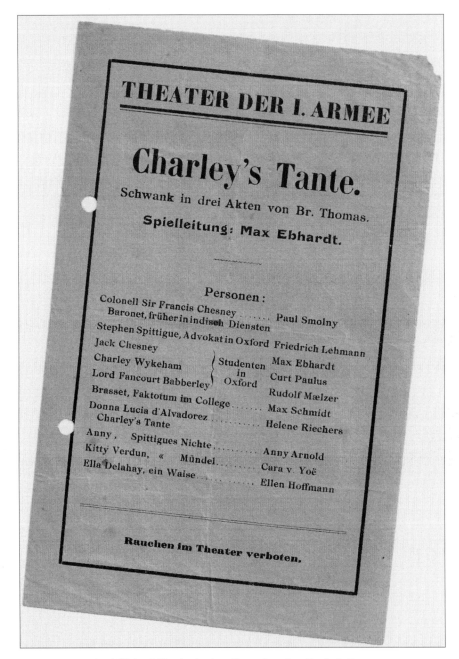

Playbill for "Charley's Aunt" produced at Rethel, France
for the First Army, undated.

Chapter 3

Defending the Republic, 1918–1921

The lie that the "November Criminals" had "stabbed Germany in the back" was so potent and so useful to right-wing groups, and especially later to the Nazi Party, that it lay unburied throughout the history of the Weimar Republic. But this fundamental falsehood belied the indisputable fact that by August 1918 First Quartermaster-General Erich Ludendorff understood that German forces could not win; by September, he was urgently pressing the Kaiser's government to secure an immediate armistice. General Ludendorff, an immediate casualty of his request, was replaced on October 29 by General Wilhelm Groener.[1]

That very afternoon, General Groener reached an understanding with Friedrich Ebert, the head of the Social Democratic Party and the president of the newly proclaimed republic, that the military would support the new government provided it did not seek to reform the traditional officer corps. The fledgling republic now had an army, but with a price: it found itself hostage to the military. As a noted historian of the Weimar Republic concluded, "one may well regret this decision—and the further history of the German Republic gives every reason to

regret it—but one cannot deny its sheer necessity."[2]

But although the army marched back into Germany in a disciplined manner and pledged through General Groener a conditional loyalty to the new government, that did not mean that Germany was free from the threat of violence and disorder coming from thousands of armed and displaced veterans as well as from civilians seeking a new order. After four years of total war and the deep shock and agony of unexpected defeat, coupled with the severe hunger of the German people brought on by the continued Allied blockade, it was of little wonder that war's seldom separated twin, revolution, should quickly manifest itself. As early as November 4, "the red flag flew from every ship in northern ports."[3] But what would be the nature of these revolutionary movements, and how comprehensive and lasting would be their effects?

In 1918 and 1919, while there was a multiplicity of political parties, it would not be much of an oversimplification to suggest there was only one basic choice as to the republic's direction and the future of the revolution which had brought it into being: either a majority popular democracy or a Bolshevik style of dictatorship of the proletariat. The fundamental question was whether a political revolution replacing the Second Reich with truly democratic institutions would be sufficient to preserve those institutions, or would a thorough and comprehensive revolution modeled on Bolshevik Russia—a revolution which transformed that country's economy and its basic institutions—be necessary to prevent any attempt to restore the old regime and thus nullify any gains made through the political revolution?[4]

This profound issue created a tumultuous atmosphere which affected nearly the entire population, whether traditional elites, urban and rural workers, or demobilized soldiers and sailors of every rank. Although a minority of socialists were committed to the Bolshevik model as the only way to go beyond a political revolution to achieve proletarian rule and to forestall reactionary politics, the vast majority, tired of war and revolution (even those supposedly socialist members of the Social Democratic Party), chose to support the republic and the forces of law and order. My father was among the majority who chose to protect the newly proclaimed republic against threats which he believed emanated primarily from the revolutionary Bolshevik left.

The nature, outlook, organization, and allegiance of these "forces of law and order" varied greatly. Under the generic name *Freikorps* (Free Corps), well over a hundred paramilitary groups sprang into being. Many, if not most of these, were as opposed to the republic as they were to the Bolsheviks and the revolutionary left. The ideology of their leaders more often ran in a reactionary, monarchist direction and, later, many members of these *Freikorps* units would buy into Nazi ideology.

Indeed, Nigel Jones entitled his interesting study, *Hitler's Heralds: The Story of the Freikorps 1918–1922*.[5]

It remains a controversial issue as to whether the *Freikorps* movement represented a continuation of the First World War into the subsequent postwar revolution, or whether it looked instead to the future as a harbinger of Nazism. In a recent article, Ben Scott argued that the *Freikorps* eschewed political goals in favor of direct action and that a shift to Nazi ideology occurred only after the dissolution of the *Freikorps*.[6]

Historian Richard Watt rejects the idea of a monolithic *Freikorps* movement. Watt's general conclusion is that the effect of the *Freikorps* on the Weimar Republic "was a corrosive and destructive one" and that they "constituted an endless threat to the Republic and to the lives of its principal officials." But Watt makes a distinction between an old and a new *Freikorps*.[7]

Watt rejects the idea that all *Freikorps* were "ultra-reactionary gangs formed of white-guard types." Instead, he suggests that "a high degree of initiative, flexibility and imagination" would have been required of these earlier units.[8] He asserts that early *Freikorps* units were made up of regiments of the former imperial army and that their members thought of themselves as belonging to that former army. On the other hand, Watt believes, members of the later *Freikorps* units "had to start from scratch" and recruiting them was more difficult because "the best of the old army privates and non-commissioned officers had already joined the Freikorps."[9]

In the appendix of his book on *The Reichswehr and the German Republic*, Professor Harold Gordon analyzed 146 of the *Freikorps* organized in 1918 and 1919. Of these, 11 are in his first category,

GERMANY

National Border   City   Regional Border

"*Freikorps* led by the Generals." For Gordon, it is not a question of "old vs. new" *Freikorps* but rather one of leadership. Those *Freikorps* led by generals, Gordon concludes, were organized so as to ultimately incorporate them, "into the new army of the Reich."[10]

While admitting that some early *Freikorps* units held ultra-nationalist and racist ideas, this was more evident in later *Freikorps* organizations in contrast to those formed and led by generals which were, because of their discipline and size, "well-qualified" to be later integrated into the *Vorläufige Reichswehr* (Provisional National Defense).[11]

It was General Groener who, on December 6, 1918, agreed that volunteers under the command of former imperial officers could be used to suppress street fighting and riots in Berlin often involving members of the Independent Social Democratic Party of Germany (*Unabhängige Sozialdemokratische Partei Deutschlands—USPD*) and/or Spartacists who, after January 1, adopted the formal name Communist Party of Germany (*Kommunistische Partei Deutschlands—KPD*).[12]

On December 12, General Georg Maercker, a commander of the former 214th Infantry Division, submitted a plan for the creation of a *Freikorps* unit. The *Freiwilliges Landesjägerkorps* (*FLJK*) was formed December 14 and, as such, became the first *Freikorps* to be officially recognized by the government of the republic.[13]

Although General Maercker was a convinced monarchist, he required all his volunteers to take an oath of loyalty to the republic, and he purged undisciplined troops from his organization. As a further inducement to join, Maercker arranged for music and sports programs for his men as well as providing training in vocational skills. Among the Rempe papers there is one which listed track and field events and which named him as one of the official timekeepers for the meet.[14] These programs and opportunities, in addition to the daily pay of one mark, led to rapid enlistment, so that by the end of December 1918 Maercker's *Freikorps* numbered about 4,000 men.[15]

By early January 1919, *Reichspräsident* Friedrich Ebert and his Minister of Defense Gustav Noske could feel a sense of relief as they reviewed ranks of disciplined soldiers at a military camp outside Berlin. Ebert's government had recently asked General Maercker to place his troops under the command of General Walther von Lüttwitz for the defense and security of Berlin. At the military review, Gustav Noske reputedly assured President Ebert that he could rest easy, "as everything is going to be alright from now on."[16] My father, who enlisted in Maercker's FLJK on December 18, was in the ranks of those who marched in review past Friedrich Ebert and Gustav Noske on that cold January day.[17]

My father's motives for joining Maercker's *FLJK* were not so different from the many others who did so. Ben Scott, in his previously cited article, noted that "some 25% of the junior officers joined the Freikorps."[18] Richard Watt does not challenge this figure, arguing that the end of the war meant officers "were stripped of privilege, rank, profession and prestige." Watt states: "prior to 1914 it was said that the young Lieutenant went through life as a god, the Lieutenant of Reserves as a demi-god."[19] Many of those who joined were of middle-class origin, many joined for the material benefits, and many joined from a spirit of patriotism, a desire for action and a fear of a Russian-inspired Bolshevik revolution.

While differing at several points on the nature of the *Freikorps*, Waite and Jones agree that General Maercker's *FLJK* was unique among the many *Freikorps* organizations. Waite points out that Maercker's corps "was characterized by strict discipline moderation and military bearing beyond reproach," and he concludes that other *Freikorps* units thought the *FLJK* was "woefully lacking in the freebooter spirit."[20]

Jones arrives at a similar assessment: "not for Maercker was the brutal neo-anarchic 'free booting spirit' so manifest in other more notorious examples of the *Freikorps* genre."[21] A similar conclusion may be found in the earlier work of Professor Harold Gordon, who asserts that "Maercker's Freikorps, unlike some others, was a model of discipline and restraint." He goes even further, arguing that "the Weimar Republic owed a very considerable debt of gratitude to [Maercker], who accomplished so much with so very little bloodshed."[22]

Given these distinctive attributes of the *FLJK*, it is not very surprising that "many men of liberal convictions enlisted" in Maercker's unit. As the *FLJK* grew rapidly in numbers, it acquired, in addition to machine guns and trench mortars, "light and heavy artillery, flame throwers, armored cars and even aircraft."[23] Thus the *FLJK* became a self-sufficient fighting unit, and, as one of the better organized, trained, and disciplined *Freikorps* units, it was frequently used by the republican

government to suppress vicious street fighting, riots, and other forms of civil strife.[24]

In Berlin, the principal threat in those early January days came from the Spartacists, a revolutionary group of not many more than a thousand individuals who were led by a brilliant communist theoretician, Rosa Luxemburg, and her more volatile colleague Karl Liebknecht. While reluctant to proclaim the advent of the proletarian revolution, Luxemburg and others called for a general strike on January 5, 1919. This uprising—"Spartacus Week" —was put down by January 11, and it was the *FLJK* of General Maercker that had a major role in restoring order.[25] In his 1956 memoir, my father recalled how "Berlin was in turmoil . . . bloodshed and violence were the order of the day and it was dangerous to go in uniform on the streets."[26]

In that same memoir, my father claimed to have been in Berlin on January 19, "conferring with General von Lüttwitz at the Eden Hotel when I saw Karl Liebknecht and Rosa Luxemburg, two communist leaders, being shot before my eyes."[27] However, my father's memoir has the wrong date since those two brilliant and charismatic revolutionary leaders were brutally beaten and murdered by members of the Horse Guards Division on January 15. In a book on the Spartacist Uprising, Dr Eric Waldman speculates that had these two leaders lived, they "might have prevented the Russian Bolsheviks from becoming the controlling power of the German Communist Movement."[28]

Dr Werner Angress also condemns their murder and adds that with the death of Rosa Luxemburg, "the movement began to lose the humanitarian spirit and idealism which had governed and motivated its actions in the past."[29]

On the other hand, there is no doubt that my father was in Berlin during this period of intense turmoil. His papers preserve a January 13 order, issued from Paderborn, which transferred him from his wartime flight unit, *Flieger-Abteilung (Artillerie) 261*, to *Flieger-Abteilung 18* of the *FLJK* and ordering him to Berlin's Tempelhof Airport to help in the organization of a flying squadron.[30] He also kept a blue identification card, noted as "number 6," which was signed by Minister of Defense Gustav Noske. The card bears a picture of Leonhard wearing his war medals and in the uniform of the *FLJK*. The ID card notes that the bearer is entitled to carry weapons and asks that he be given full support from all military authorities. Besides Noske's signature, the card is signed by Captain and Aircraft Leader Victor Krocker. On the back of the card my father's monthly re-enlistment dates are given from April 15 to July 15, 1919.[31] On January 22, from Tetlow (a town between Berlin and Potsdam), *Leutnant der Reserve* Rempe is identified as a pilot of *Flieger-Abteilung 423* belonging to the flying squadrons of General von Lüttwitz.[32]

Prior to this date, on January 19 the government held elections to the National Constituent Assembly. The Social Democratic Party was the big winner with nearly 40 percent of the vote, while the Communist Party boycotted the election. By the end of January, the government decided it could be better protected in Weimar, a small town about 140 miles (225km) southwest of Berlin. Weimar not only provided improved security, but it

also suggested ideals more suited to the new republic; after all, had it not been at varying times the home of Goethe and Schiller?[33]

General Maercker encountered unexpected resistance in securing Weimar as the new capitol. On February 3, my father received orders to fly an LVG C.VI (No. 7692/18) from Tetlow to Weimar in support of General Maercker. Once again, this order noted that the pilot possessed a license to carry weapons and it requested that *Leutnant der Reserve* Rempe "receive unhindered support from all officials and military officers as well as from Soldiers' and Workers' Councils especially in case of an emergency landing." The order was signed for "the Council" by Sergeant Gorbel and by Victor Krocker, Captain and Detachment Commander.[34] By early February General Maercker's men had encircled and secured the new capitol city of Weimar.

On February 6 the National Constituent Assembly met in its first session to draft a constitution. But this did not mean that peace, law, and order had come to Germany. On February 11, for example, there were major strikes and riots in Gotha, and these were not suppressed by the *FLJK* until February 20. Two days later, "Ltn. Rempe of Flying Detachment 423 (Krocker)" received an order to transport four Fokker D.VIIs from the *Fliegerersatzabteilung* in Gotha.[35]

By February 27 civil order in central Germany was on the edge of complete collapse as vital rail and communication links between Weimar and Berlin were disrupted and strikes and counterstrikes became more common. Minister of Defense Noske—"The Bloodhound of the Revolution"—now ordered General Maercker to pacify the important city of Halle by putting an end to strikes, violence, and anarchy that were almost consuming the city. Initially, Maercker sought to avoid violence, but a scheduled meeting with the local Soldiers' and Workers' Councils never occurred; in fact, Maercker had to take refuge in the Post Office in order to avoid the revolutionary mobs.[36]

As an officer in the *FLJK*, undoubtedly my father shared the opinion of a writer in the *Saale-Zeitung* newspaper that the *FLJK* was "the only reason the Spartacists in Halle were unable to hatch their plan of going from house to house, robbing, burning, and murdering."[37]

Although Halle remained under martial law until the end of March, my father received this order on March 5: "Leutnant Rempe and Assistant Medical Director, Dr. Bruns, in plane LVG.C.VI 7692/18, to fly to Paderborn for professional duties." The order was signed from the Weimar airport by Captain Victor Krocker.[38] Twenty years later to the month of the signing of the 1918 Armistice, Dr Bruns presided as my father's best man at his wedding in Milwaukee, Wisconsin, in November 1938.

On March 6, my father was provided a permit which identified him as a member of the Flier Detachment 423 of the Voluntary Provincial Light Infantry Corps. The permit allowed him to carry a weapon and noted that "Ltn. Rempe is housed in Weimar and is permitted to move about the city." The street address was intentionally left blank. Nine days later my father was at the library to check out Ernst von Wildenbruch's *Das Hohelied von Weimar*. Apparently the Weimar library was less concerned about his security, as they listed his address as Leidenberg No. 6.[39]

My father made his home in Weimar for the next two years. Although the following text bears no date, it is likely that Ferdinand Grafemann's *Landesjäger in Weimar* comes from this period.

Following our long hard service we stroll through the streets of our town and hope that friendly thoughts and warm looks on us rain down.

We have set ourselves a great goal: training soldiers, true soldiers, from naught no easy task, yet we have no doubts, we'll reach the goal we've sought.

And so our bold anthem floats out, sweet German girls, from window and door: We are the future, moving ever forward, Fear and Death will be no more.[40]

Riots, violence, strikes, and civil disorder continued to erupt in Germany in April and May. The government's reliance on various *Freikorps* units, including those more brutal than General Maercker's *FLJK*, often incited left-wing resistance. Professor Jones notes that while the *FLJK* fought hard against those who challenged the law and order policies of the Weimar government, "its relative bloodlessness is a tribute to Maercker's own insistence on discipline, and moderation. Unfortunately this attitude was to prove atypical of the general Freikorps mentality."[41]

Some of the military discipline insisted upon by General Maercker can be inferred from the following order from Captain Victor Krocker. The order announces that General Maercker would soon review the detachment:

1. All planes [12 LVGs] will be flight ready in front of hangers; the Fokker group in front of the tents. In case of questionable weather, Captain Krocker is to be asked whether or not to prepare the planes.
2. Hangers, tents, and workshops are to be cleaned.
3. Everything in the depots should be stowed in an orderly manner. Accounting books (received and shipped) should be laid out for viewing.
4. Fuel reserves and canisters should be neatly arranged. Fuel and other logbooks should be ready for review.[42]

On the day of this order, a general strike began in Magdeburg, and the *FLJK* was ordered to occupy the city. On April 12, Leonhard received orders to fly a Fokker D.VII (No. 8448/18) from Weimar to Magdeburg and return; as before, he possessed a license which permitted him to carry weapons. Two days later he took off from Magdeburg with two other Fokker D.VII aircraft but had to make an emergency landing at Halle because of rain and thick fog. Taking off immediately from Halle, he had to make another emergency landing at Krosigk since a piece of the plane's propeller came off during takeoff.[43]

Only the best and most trustworthy *Freikorps* were to be absorbed into the *Vorläufige Reichswehr* (Provisional National Defense); accordingly, on May 2, 1919 General Maercker's *FLJK* was dissolved to become part of the new *Reichswehr-Brigade 16*. My father experienced early action in the Weimar Republic's army when General Maercker was sent to Leipzig on May 7 to secure that important city for the government. Two days later, my father signed up for a

three-month period as a member of the *Vorläufige Reichswehr*.[44] After martial law was declared in Leipzig, my father was required to make several flights between Weimar and Leipzig between May 17 and June 10.[45]

On June 24, he received a request from the military airfield at Halle stating: "the Detachment is in dire need of approximately ten sets of maps of Germany, on a scale of 1:200 [colored flying maps]. Above all, it is important that we receive as many sets as possible of the pages for Erfurt, Halle, Magdeburg, Leipzig, and Görlitz. There should be a great many maps still in stock at the airfield . . . the Detachment could also use one of the map cabinets in store there."[46]

Looking toward his future, my father made the following request with ration stamps attached:

Leutnant Rempe, Artillery Flying Squadron 116 Military Brigade 16, Weimar, requests to buy: 3.4m coat fabric (brown) @ 18.25 marks per meter = 62.05 marks, lining material for one shirt = 11.18 marks, lining material for one pair of pants = 2.66 marks

Captain and Squadron Commander Victor Krocker authorized this request with the notation, "Leutnant Rempe will be discharged soon and is in dire need of a civilian suit."[47]

Although he lived in Weimar for two years, my father's papers record only one visit to the National Constituent Assembly. He took from that meeting a copy of a motion which requested the Reichstag's president "to study the viability of making stenographic reports of the National Assembly available free of charge in reading rooms, libraries, and other educational establishments . . . so that every citizen can have access to it."[48]

The day of discharge arrived: September 20, 1919. My father's discharge papers read as follows:

Rank: Leutnant of the Reich
First and last name: Leonhard Rempe
Birth date and place: June 30, 1893, Driburg
Field Division: Mounted Division . . . 35
Discharged: September 20, 1919 in Driburg.[49]

One week later an announcement came which dissolved *Artillery Flying Squadron 116.* Dated September 27, Brigade Orders No. 1 read:

Artillery Flying Squadron is transferred under the order of Army Group Command II, Kassel . . . Herewith the Artillery Flying Squadron leaves the organizations of the National Rifle Corps which it had belonged to since inception as Flier Detachment 423.

This leaves me to give my particular recognition to the Squadron, from its duty-conscious leader, but also the untiring crews and finally the entire ground personnel for their work for the *Landesjägerkorps.*

The success with which the division mastered many difficulties, with which the flying service must cope at the moment, should be particularly emphasized, in other words, shortages and poor availability of materials and fuel, as well as the general political situation.

Through 1,049 flights, with a total flying distance of 212,052 km [131,763

miles], the Squadron performed outstanding service, when it was needed to quickly restore needed transportation lines for the *Landesjägerkorps* . . . My best wishes accompany Flier Escort Krocker in their further future.

In farewell, I wish the leaders and the crews a heartfelt good luck.

Signed: Maercker

With the validity of the signature attested to by Krocker, Captain and Escort Leader.[50]

We do not hear from *Leutnant* Rempe until March 1920. An identification card states: "*Leutnant* Rempe is a volunteer in the service of the *Polizei Flieger Staffel* [Police Squadron], and is thus permitted to enter the barracks of the group." The card, from Paderborn, is dated March 22.[51]

Interestingly, March 22 was the very date in which Minister of Defense Gustav Noske was forced to resign his post in the wake of the failed Kapp Putsch that March. Neither my father's 1956 memoir nor the papers he preserved in his archive provide any information about the Kapp Putsch or about the subsequent bloody suppression of the Ruhr Uprising, which was not overcome until early April 1920.

In fact, the remaining papers in his archive are mostly concerned with securing benefits for medical care. In November 1920, for instance, the Benefits Office at Paderborn wrote to him:

This is to inform you that your request for reimbursement of the costs for medical care (submitted on November 19) has been submitted and is already being processed. However, whether or not the request can be processed as you wish is

not yet clear; you should have consulted
this office before treatment, so that the
pre-existing approval could be acquired
from the Central Benefits Office in
Münster. In the future, you should first
consult with that Benefits Office.[52]

He was still pursuing his claim in June
the following year, as indicated by a letter
sent from the Benefits Office at Paderborn
dated June 4, 1921. This letter is addressed
to "Herr Businessman Leonhard Rempe"
and was delivered to Alhausen near
Driburg.[53]

The rest of my father's story is
autobiographical in nature and is told in his
1956 memoir. Unfortunately, there is no
independent source to confirm his very
human action (no date given) when the
time came to surrender his plane to the
French in fulfillment of the Versailles
Treaty:

> When the day came, our few planes
> were lined up on the field. Before the
> French Commission arrived, I took my
> old Fokker D.VII once more to the air,
> and when I saw the Frenchmen arrive in
> their motor cavalcade I came in for a
> landing; and before I touched the
> ground I made purposely a complete
> crack-up, got out of the wreckage,
> saluted stiffly the French colonel who in
> turn did the same, however a little
> bewildered, and then I left the field
> proud but sad. Another chapter in my
> life was closing.[54]

Chapter 3 Photos

General Georg Maercker (central figure facing the camera), the founder and commander of the
Freiwilliges Landesjägerkorps (FLJK).

Minister of Defense Gustav Noske reviewing members of the *Freiwilliges Landesjägerkorps.*

An inspection of members of the *Freiwilliges Landesjägerkorps* in January 1919.

Civilians inspecting an LVG (Luft-Verkehrs-Gesellschaft) C.VI
reconnaissance plane of the *Freiwilliges Landesjägerkorps*. Gustav Noske
appears in the white hat.

The *Flugplatz* (airfield) at Weimar.

Leonhard Rempe as a member of General Maercker's *Freiwilliges Landesjägerkorps.*

The high jump—an *FLJK* sports competition at Weimar.

The relay race during an *FLJK* sports competition at Weimar.

Dr Bruns, assistant medical director of
Flieger-Abteilung 18.

Pilots from *Flieger-Abteilung 423*, from left to right: Ozineck, Muller, Munichow, Kohne,
Kronmann, Herbst, Wrensh, Aue, Hasselmann, Huninghaus, Viereck, Rempe,
Schwamm, Griedewald, and Welkoborsky.

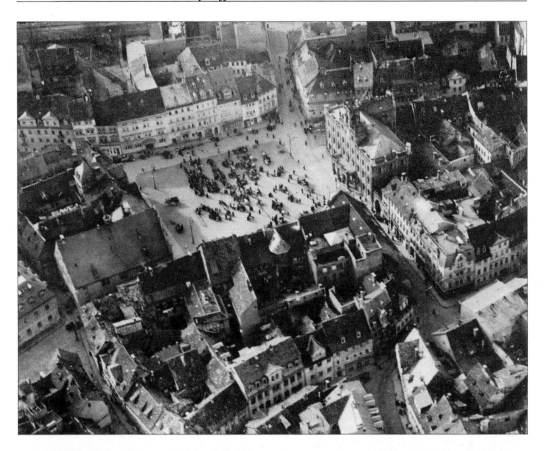

Einteilung des Geschäftsdienstes der Flg.Abt.423
Führer: Hauptmann KROCKER   Abt VIII (Revierstube)

Abt. I. Geschäftswesen	Abt. II. Kassenwesen	Abt. III. Techn. Abtlg.	Abt. IV. Bild-Abt.	Abt. V. F.T.Abt.	Abt. VI. Waffen u. Bomben	Abt. VII. Wirtschafts-Abt.	Abt. VIII. Gesundheitswesen

Organization chart for *Flieger-Abteilung 423*. Leonhard Rempe was in charge of *Abt.III.*

Opposite page

Top: An aerial view of a street demonstration against the Weimar Republic.

Bottom: *Polizei Flieger Staffel* (Police Squadron), Paderborn. Leonhard Rempe is seated on the wheel of the aircraft.

Iz. Flieg. Staff. Padeborn. 8. II. 20. Essen–Krupp. H. = 2500. Br.= 50 cm

The Krupp works in Essen, the heartland of German arms manufacturing.

Opposite page

The final photo in Leonhard Rempe's war album, showing him in full uniform.

ID document dated November 29, 1918. Issued by the
Local Soldiers and Workers Council in Driburg.

This ID document, dated February 3, 1919 indicates that Ltn Rempe
is a member of *Flying Detachment Number 23*.

Rempe in his uniform as a member of General Maercker's *Freikorps* unit. The ID is signed number 6 by Minister of Defense, G Noske.

Document from Captain and Detachment Commander Victor Krocker to Rempe ordering him to Gotha to pick up four Fokker DVIIs.

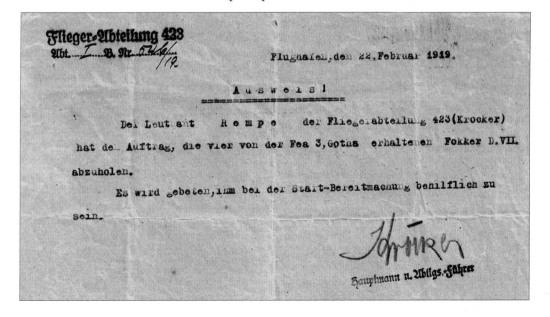

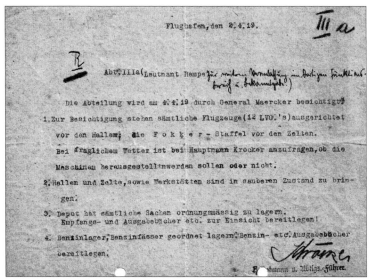

Document from Victor Krocker dated April 2, 1919 stating that
General Maercker will be arriving to review the flight detachment.

Library card issued in Weimar, March 15, 1919, stating that Rempe
has checked out a book by Ernst Wildenbruch.

Chapter 4

The 1956 Memoir

My father wrote the following brief memoir during the early winter months of 1956 at the age of 63. In a very real sense, it was his last testament, for he died later that year in September.

Reproduced here are the first 20 pages of a 26-page document. The remaining six pages describe his life and family in the United States as well as his worldwide travels until 1956. Clearly, he wanted his wife and three children—I was 14 at the time—to have a better understanding of his boyhood in Germany and, most importantly, his varied experiences during the First World War and its immediate aftermath.

This memoir differs at several points from the unfinished one he penned in 1930, including the fact that this work was written in English, his adopted second language, while the 1930 memoir was written in German. I decided not to edit his prose, so that readers will have a better sense of his use of English.

The final chapter of this book considers how my father's last memoir relates to the many historical documents that form the basis for the first three chapters of this book.

* * *

Foreword

Es war einmal, so fangen alle Märchen an.[1]

This however is not a fairy tale but a true account of my life, which so far I have enjoyed very much. According to insurance statistics the space of a man's life is sixty-five years so it's about time I tell you all I know about the man who became your father by divine destiny, or by accident. Soon I will be sixty-three years old and looking back on my life I must say it has been wonderful and I am grateful to the Lord.

Chapter 1

It was a sunny day, Friday, June 30th, 1893 when I was born. The place was a little pleasant town, Bad Driburg in Westphalia, Germany, where my grandparents lived. My father, Karl Rempe, was a magistrate in the Federal Government. He was a wonderful man and father who had many interests in life. He played the piano rather well and had a beautiful voice. Father loved the outdoors, and was an ardent fisherman, a great gardener and was known for feeding stations which he set up in the winter for birds all through Germany. Father died rather young in Warburg when I was nine years old. My father came from an old family of jurists. His father had been an attorney and his grandfather also. Father had two brothers, Ludwig, who became a doctor, and Joseph, who studied for the priesthood, was ordained, and went to the U.S.A. and died in Illinois at eighty-nine years old. There were also two girls in the family that became nuns.

My good mother, her maiden name was Josephine Waldeyer, came from a very old Westphalian farm family. She devoted her whole life to her children, Karl, Margaret, Leonhard and Josie. She died in Oberhunden in the last days of the war in March, 1945.

Mother's family had been large, four girls and two boys. Mother was the oldest. The next was her brother Leonhard who was an Army Surgeon with the rank of a General; he was, by the. way, my godfather. After him came Mimi who married Doctor of Medicine Richard Bruning in Lippstadt, west of Paderborn. The next girl, Antonie, married Franz Schröder, who had a beautiful farm near Paderborn. Joseph, the next boy, went into the lumber business and the youngest one, a girl, Emilie, married Dr. Joseph Monniker in Nieheim, north east of Bad Driburg and from all of them I inherited many cousins. The family clan of the Waldeyers was a very close one, and they all stick together as it should be.

The smartest of us children was my brother Karl. Learning came easy to him. He was studying shipbuilding and engineering in Berlin and Charlottenburg when the war broke out. He, of course, too served his country, became an officer in the infantry and fought bravely in the war on both fronts. He was wounded on the Western Front and after the war he studied

theology in Innsbruck, Austria, and became a priest, and I believe a good one. He took mother as a housekeeper, served again in the Hitler war and is now pastor in Nieheim, Westphalia.

My sister, Margaret, was perhaps the best of us children. She left Germany in 1913, came to America and was for many years housekeeper for my uncle Joseph. She died in the year 1941, in Chicago, beloved and missed by all who knew her. Josie, the youngest one, married a farmer, Albert Schulte-Potthoff, had one daughter, Liselotte, and is living on their farm near Soest.

My childhood could not have been better; I remember only a few tears but lots of laughter. My school years, however, as a whole were miserable. My teachers were old men who did not seem to understand me. I went to four different schools and in between I had a tutor and one governess. The long summer vacations were the highlights in this period. While our father lived we spent those golden days on the seashore of the Baltic Sea or travelling through Italy. Later I spent my vacation with my cousins on large farms, which belonged to relatives. We helped with the harvest, rode the horses, hunted a great deal and had much fun. Finally, I graduated with some sort of honor and wanted to become a forester. Before I took this step I made long trips on my bicycle through the mountains of Germany and it was on such a trip through the Harz Mountains when the fatal shot in Sarajevo, on June 28th, 1914, was heard around the world.

Chapter 2

The *casus belli* was there and in spite of efforts to avoid conflict, war broke out and the date was August 1st, 1914. I was in Berlin on that day and heard the German Kaiser Wilhelm II say from the balcony of his castle, "I do not know any German parties, I only know Germans."

Now a chapter started in my life and it was an eventful one. I left my childhood and became a man. Needless to say I felt like every good German, and thought we were fighting a just war. I looked for a regiment to join preferably the cavalry and this was not an easy task. Men and horses were already on the Western Front or fighting on the eastern border. However, after a few weeks, I found in West Prussia in the town of Deutsch-Eylau a Field Artillery regiment. I was accepted in the *Riding Horse Artillery Regiment #35,*[2] and I was extremely happy.

After a few months of rugged training in the military, exercising and shooting with the field cannons and horsemanship, we went over to Memel into the Russian war zone where we joined the 2nd Cavalry Division and the war began for me in earnest. Soon I received the baptism of fire, but for me it still was fun chasing the Russians like rabbits all over the fields and steppes and tundras. In the spring of 1915, I was made a corporal and in the summer I advanced to be a sergeant. We went through Lithuania, Kurland, Ostland, always on the move. Luck played a great role in my life and especially in the war.

Here is what happened to me in mid-October, 1915. We were engaged in a fierce battle with the Russians. Our cannons were in positions and firing. My Commanding Officer and I were in advanced positions, directing and observing the shooting. We were both lying in shallow holes, which I had quickly dug,

the captain giving orders and I with the field telephone relaying the commands to the battery. We were under heavy fire from the enemy cannons, machine guns and infantry fire. We could clearly see that our shells did a great deal of harm to the Russians, when all of a sudden repeating an order from my captain the telephone line went dead. To repair the phone I quickly took the wire and ran and crawled under heavy enemy fire back to the battery. Our cannons of course were silent but halfway back we were shooting again. I turned around and ran as quickly as possible back to our outpost where I heard the captain give orders through the field phone. He was happy and so was I, and when evening came we had the enemy on the run and the battle was won. Thanks to me as everyone said, even if I had not done a darn thing except perhaps that the wires had a short somewhere and I, running back with the lines in my hand, had eliminated the short and restored the connection. Anyway, I was to report to the Commanding Officer at night, which I did.

He gave me the coveted Iron Cross Second Class and told me to leave in the morning for Berlin and report to the famous Artillery School, Jüterbog, for further learning and promotion if I would pass the necessary examinations. Who was happier than I leaving the war, going to Berlin and seeing pretty girls again? Early next morning I rode on horseback to the nearest railway station sixty kilometers away, boarded a train and was on my way to becoming an officer and a gentleman.

I reported in due time at the school where I and many aspirants from other Artillery regiments, all fine boys, who were willing to give their lives *pro patria* but before that they wanted to have some fun and who could blame them. And fun we had. For me it was a glorious time. Since the school did not appeal to me—no one ever did—particularly this one with its higher mathematics and ballistics, I seldom attended and spent most of my time in Berlin where I visited often a brother of my grandfather's, Dr. Wilhelm von Wald-eyer–Hartz, who was a professor at the University of Berlin, a very famous anatomist who is known all over the world, at least in medical circles, for his identification of the Waldeyer Ring[3] and other accomplishments in his field. We had many interesting discussions and my social calendar was always filled. These months in Berlin I will never forget as they were very pleasant. All good things come to an end and so did this one. The day of reckoning and the final examinations were coming and lady luck was with me once again.

Chapter 3

It was a cold morning when we all assembled at the shooting and proving grounds—students were present and standing at attention before a general, a few colonels and other brass. I was a little nervous when the general looked hard at me with his piercing cold blue eyes and said, "Rempe, there somewhere in the distance is a machine gun nest and here is a battery of four cannons at your disposal. Knock that gun out of action." I kicked sharply my heels, took command of the battery, spotted through my glasses the object far away and with my loudest voice gave the command to fire with one cannon at a certain distance. I observed the shot a little to the side and about five hundred

yards in front of the target. I made the necessary corrections and the second shot was in the direct line but five hundred yards behind the target. Now making the right deduction, I directed the four cannons of the battery on the target, commanded fire and the machine gun nest was instantly obliterated. The general congratulated me and dispensed me from all other oral examinations, which were, as I know, very tough.

After a celebration with my comrades I said goodbye to Jüterbog and Berlin and left for a furlough, which I spent with my mother. After this I was to report again to my old regiment which was somewhere in Russia, and I found it somewhere in Poland.

The joy to be back again with where I belonged even when some of the best were gone, either killed or wounded, was great. By that time, the moving war had shifted to a static one. Both sides were in trenches and we lived in dugouts. The winters in Russia were very cold and miserable, lots of snow and it was often twenty to thirty degrees below zero. Many a would-be conqueror like Charles II of Sweden, Napoleon, and later Hitler found that out and was beaten by the Russian ally, General Winter.

The front was little active and, as a whole, was all quiet on the Eastern Front. Nevertheless, we had a good time. We took troikas, Russian sleds drawn by a team of three horses abreast, visited neighboring cavalry regiments, played cards, poker, bridge and skat, and had many glasses of steaming grog, that is a little hot tea with lots of rum.

One night, it was January 14th, 1916, I was on duty and patrol in the trenches close to the enemy. In fact, so close that I could hear in the clear cold night the Russian soldiers sing their sad songs and play their balalaikas when I got a phone call from H.Q. that the Kaiser had given me a commission as a Lieutenant. I was at once relieved of my duties and reported to H.Q. There my comrades awaited me with a big hello— congratulations, and champagne were in order and we were celebrating till the late morning hours. Now I was a full-fledged officer. A gentleman I had been all my life, but now it was official.

With my commission came new duties. I was at once attached to the staff of the regiment. My main duty was to keep the colonel in good humor, ride the horses and take care of the logistics. The winter passed, spring came in with thaw and mud, and the war started moving again. In May, 1916, I was transferred as a liaison officer to an Austrian corps and was attached to a general who was the commander of a Hungarian Cavalry brigade, the Honvéd Hussars. The Austrian and Hungarian officers were charming men, and I had great pleasure riding their blooded horses, playing whist, bridge, poker and drinking their golden wine, Tokayer.

Chapter 4

But the strength of the Russian Army was almost broken. I was looking to the West and to heroic deeds, so I decided to train as a pilot, join the Air Force and do some fighting over the Western Front. The Air Force was relatively new, pilots were wanted and so I put in my application, said *adieu* to my comrades and left for Germany to visit my mother. After a few weeks a telegram called me to the Luftwaffe. One of the training centers was in Breslau. I reported there to the

commanding officer, it was summer 1916, and I asked to be trained as a pilot.[4] The C.O. looked surprised, said a firm "no" and told me that since I was an artillerist to train as an observer. As I said just as firmly "no" to his proposition, he got real mad and annoyed with me and was ready to throw me out when the door opened and a tall captain from the Life Hussars with a big silver skull and crossbones on his headgear came in.

The Commanding Officer, who had an even higher rank, stood at stiff attention and stammered, "Imperial Highness." The Imperial Highness ignored him, temporarily came over to me, put his arm around me and said, "Rempe how wonderful to see you, now we can train here together as pilots and fight together in the West." It happened that this particular Imperial Highness was an old friend of mine, Prince Friedrich Karl von Preussen, a nephew of the Kaiser, with whom I had fought in the same battles in Russia.

Needless to say, I got, at once, permission to train as a pilot and left with the prince in his car for Hundsfeld, a small town near Breslau where pilots were trained. It took the prince one month to complete his training. He had an instructor and two machines at his disposal. It took me three months to complete the course because forty other officers and I had one instructor and one airplane. We had a big farewell dinner for the prince, and I had to promise that I would come to his squadron in France after my course was completed, but fate interfered. Prince Friedrich Karl was killed within a few weeks while flying over France. He was a gallant officer and a real Hohenzoller.

My training went on; I met many wonderful men there and all through the Air

Force including Baron Manfred von Richthofen, the greatest ace in that war, along with [Max] Immelmann, [Oswald] Boelcke, and many others. They were all heroes and later in France I met in the air the gallant men like Captain [Georges] Guynemer from the French Escadrille who was killed September 11th, 1917. Of him you will hear later. Other French pilots were [Adolphe] Pégoud, [René] Fonck, [Armand] de Turenne and famous among the British were Captain [Douglas] Bell, and Major [Lanoe] Hawker, and the Americans were well represented by Captain Eddie Rickenbacker. We respected each other, friend or foe.

My training as a pilot finally came to a successful end and if people ask me what has been the greatest single moment in my life I say without doubt or hesitation, my solo flight. It is really wonderful when you take off all by yourself for the first time without anybody to help you, just you and the plane in the blue sky. You are completely on your own—only God as your co-pilot. After the solo flight of course came training in the finer art of flying which in time I learned to master. When I was ready I went home again to mother and waited for my new assignment: I did not have to wait long.

Chapter 5

A telegram arrived calling me to the Western Front. I was ordered to report to Rethel, a little town not far from Reims, it was a rather large park for men and machines. Here I flew again with new and more modern planes and got used to the terrain. There were happy and carefree weeks. One day a captain, Count von Beroldingen, Commanding Officer of Squadron 261A[5] with the First Army, came to look me over and took me in his big Mercedes-Benz to Écly a pleasant little farm town not very far from Rethel where his squadron was located. He introduced me to his officers and assigned to me an observer, Lt. Count Julius von Soden, a man with whom I had to share the fortunes of war from now on. We became very close and this friendship lasted until 1946 when he died as a Colonel, a victim of Hitler's insane war.

The Squadron 261A was a very special one. It was strictly strategic and under the direct command of the German crown prince and the First Army. We had special-built airplanes, Rumpler C.VII with a Maybach 260 horsepower overcompressed engine, which could climb 6,000 meters in 30 minutes. Our main purpose was to photograph far beyond enemy lines, and I made many flights at great heights to Épernay, Soissons, and Paris during which my observer, Count von Soden, took pictures of the terrain, railroads, and troop movements below. Von Soden had a 50mm built-in camera besides a movie camera. Of course we only flew in perfect weather to great heights and always carried oxygen and heating equipment. Our cockpits were open, and I had two built-in machine guns which shot through the propeller, and my observer had two machine guns mounted on a pivot so that he could swing them around. The speed of the plane was about 160 kilometers per hour and an average flight could take from two to three hours.

My comrades in this squadron were wonderful men, mostly former men of the cavalry who came from the best families. There was a strong bond of friendship, we were all young, had the same ideals, and shared the same dangers. With every flight there was excitement, there was always that element of the unknown with the dogfights and air battles. Many of our brave men never returned and right here I want to say that the famous phrase "the survival of the fittest" is a fable, anyway in war. Only the best and the bravest were killed, and had I been a little braver I would not be sitting here writing this memoir.

The pictures in our squadron room changed quite often—old friends were killed and new ones took their place, "*c'est la guerre*." The spirit in our flying group, however, was high. We lived like kings in French castles, we had wonderful meals, and we sent our planes to Brussels to pick up lobsters, oysters and other delicacies including scotch and champagne, which were often the loot from our submarines. We were playing cards and had good music since many of our officers were excellent piano players with magnificent voices. We were hunting a lot in our free time as game was plenty—hares, quails, pheasants, and wild boars and deer in the Ardennes. Often we flew to Brussels were we had great holidays, in fact, we had the key to this beautiful city because the uncle of my observer, General Count von Soden, was the governor of the Belgian capital. So, all in all we were a happy lot.

When we were flying reconnaissance and taking pictures we were attacked by antiaircraft fire and enemy planes. We were not so much afraid of antiaircraft fire because at the great heights we were flying they were not very accurate. Planes, however, were another matter. As the war progressed, planes, especially fighter planes rapidly became better and faster. At the start we shot with pistols and revolvers,

shook our fists and made faces at each other but that changed with the invention of the synchronized machine gun. The Spads and Sopwiths competed with the German Fokker and were almost equal. On our flights over enemy territory we were almost always attacked, a dogfight developed and we often returned home with bullet holes through the wings and fuselage. Baron von Richthofen's plane was all red and was called the Red Knight.

The American pilot Eddie Rickenbacker had a bright hat with a ring in it on both sides of his airplane. The French ace Captain Guynemer had a flying stork painted on his aircraft and so on. My Rumpler had lightning bolts painted all over it. In that way we all knew with whom we were fighting.

Once when we came home from a long flight, March 17th, 1917,[6] a lonely Spad came out of the sun and surprised and attacked us. The pilot came diving at us and we only knew it when we heard the short bursts of a machine gun and saw tracer bullets all around us. I made a sharp curve over the wing, and as he passed us I saw to my great horror that the flying stork of Guynemer was painted over his plane. My heart sank. He was much the superior flyer, but during the dogfight I had him a couple of times in my gun sights, and so did Soden; we shot at the Spad. I just admired how Guynemer, a veteran with twenty victories, flew when all of a sudden I felt a very sharp pain in my left hand and the plane's shattered stick was now in two pieces. I grabbed what was left of the stick, pressed it forward and went down in a steep dive, with the Cathedral of Reims growing bigger and bigger, the Spad right behind us and Soden's gun still hammering away. My Rumpler started to burn; the Spad came close to us,

Guynemer waved his hand in a graceful salute and flew off in a curve.[7]

I shut off the engine to prevent the gas from blowing up the plane and managed to land in no man's land. We jumped out of the plane and ran into a crater, several French began firing at us but we made it. Soden took care of my hand as good as he could and we waited until it got dark. Then we crawled toward our lines and were soon in our own trenches. A doctor gave me a tetanus shot and at night I was brought in an ambulance to a field hospital in Rethel where they cleaned the wound in my hand.

In two weeks I was transferred to a hospital in Germany where I stayed for a few months. It was in Muskau, a beautiful castle and an old world famous park belonging to Prince Pückler. My wound healed fast, I did some knitting and took long walks in the park. All in all it was a restful time. I still had my arm in a sling when orders came to report to Braunchsweig as a flight instructor. I did not like this job at all so I wrote my old squadron requesting to call me back for duty. A telegram came fast, and I was on my way to the front.

It was nice to be back around my old comrades even if I saw many new faces. Count von Soden was happy and so was I to fly together again. The flying and fighting became more and more difficult. The air was always full of planes looking for battle and victory. I saw French planes with their blue, white and red circles on their wings, Voisin, Caudron, Breguet, and British aircraft like Handley-Page, Vickers, Bristol, Sopwith, and Spad, which stands for *Société Pour L'Aviation et ses Dérivés*. It was a circus alright.

At about this time we came to use parachutes. In order to try them and get used to them we had to make practise jumps. We were told to report to an observation balloon unit in the rear line. We went up to 1,000 feet and then we stepped out over the basket. I pulled the cord and slowly floated back down to earth. I did this only once, but it was a risky experience and fortunately I never had the occasion to do it later from a crippled or burning plane, and I am very thankful for that.

The main duties of our squadron were observation and reconnaissance. We were the eyes of the army command. Therefore, we tried to fly as high as possible, avoid fights and come home with good exposed film showing troop movements, railroad traffic, and other important information. As a whole we did a good job, and I was awarded for this with the Iron Cross First Class, which was one of the finest decorations given by the German Empire.

The year, 1918, started badly. On New Year's Day our squadron lost three planes. Four of my closest friends were killed and two, besides being badly wounded, were captured. More and more American airplanes showed up in the sky just as our resources on planes and supplies were dwindling down. But in spite of the situation our spirits were still good. I had the good fortune to see my brother, Karl, a few times. If I knew where he was in Belgium or at Verdun I flew to his place, put him in my plane, took him to our squadron and showed him a good time at our chateau. These were the highlights in this last year of the war.

The summer passed by and voices could be heard, and we saw signs that the war would be over for us in the fall without a victory on our side. It was depressing when you went home and saw the gloomy faces in Germany. The front appeared to be holding, but the German Navy, condemned to idleness, started to grumble and the idea of revolution was born there on the ships and in the harbors. Finally, under much pressure the Kaiser decided to abdicate and left the country for Holland. Prince Max von Baden took over the government and General von Hindenburg the army. President Wilson of the U.S.A. came out with his famous or infamous Fourteen Points for a just and right peace. So, on November 11th, 1918, an armistice was declared and orders came for us for an orderly march back to Germany. Firing ceased on November 11th, at 11 a.m. and the war was over and lost for us.

Our squadron got orders to fly to Gotha to deliver our machines there and to be dismissed. Soden and I climbed, for the last time, into our cockpits and flew towards the Rhine. Passing over this beautiful river, for centuries the boundary between France and Germany, a lump came up in my throat. It was hard after four years of victory to come home beaten, but we had to forget the past and look into the future. Since my gasoline was gone I had to land and with the help of some civilians I arranged to get a little supply but the gasoline was bad. I had to land twice more that day on strange fields and finally I reached Paderborn where I spent the night. I called my mother on the phone, took off the next day for Gotha, landed there, gave my machine back to the government and said, with a tear in my eye, goodbye to my friend and observer, Count Soden. We took different trains for home and the war was over for us. An important chapter in my life was now closed.

Chapter 6

Mother of course was glad to see me and so was the entire village. We did not have a word from my brother, Karl, but we knew he was somewhere in France trying to get home. He finally made it by foot and arrived on Christmas Day, 1918, thoroughly beaten and disgusted. He left right after the Christmas holidays for Innsbruck, Austria, to study theology.

I became restless and had wild plans to enter the French Foreign Legion to go to some far away island for adventure when I saw in the newspaper a proclamation by an old general who wanted volunteers to save the new government and restore order in Germany. I put on my old uniform and offered my services again. The general was glad to see so many volunteers mostly former officers and students from universities. We organized quickly and took arms, tanks, and other weapons from various depots. I had to go to Berlin, was able to find some airplanes at Tempelhof and formed a flying squadron. Berlin was in turmoil. The communists, then called Spartakists, were to take over. Bloodshed and violence were the order of the day; it was very dangerous to go in uniform out on the streets.

I was in Berlin on January 19th, 1919, conferring with General von Lüttwitz at the Eden Hotel when I saw Karl Liebknecht and Rosa Luxemburg, two communist leaders, being shot before my eyes.[8]

It got so bad in the capital that the government had to flee with our help, i.e. our newly formed volunteer army. We moved the government of the Republic to Weimar where a new constitution was framed. We stayed in Weimar two years and they were very interesting years but hectic. The new government with men like [Friedrich] Ebert, [Philipp] Scheidemann, [Gustav] Noske, [Heinrich] Brüning, all of whom I knew personally, were helpless at the start.

Germany was in a very bad way: the war was lost, the Fourteen Points completely discarded, the Peace Treaty forced upon us. Germany was in chains and almost totally helpless. Economically, the country was ruined as runaway inflation now set in. We had to see that order was restored and maintained so the government could function. We quelled riots in different places like Magdeburg, Halle, Leipzig, and Munich; unfortunately bloodshed was unavoidable. But slowly we succeeded and to some degree the rule of law began to prevail once again.

According to the 1919 Peace Treaty, the army had to dissolve itself and only a small police force was permitted. I handed in my machine when the order came to surrender all our aircraft. When that sad day arrived our few planes were lined up on the airfield. Before the French Commission arrived, I took my old Fokker D.VII once more into the air, and when I saw the Frenchmen arrive in their motor cavalcade I came in for a landing, and before I touched the ground I made purposely a complete crack-up, got out of the wreckage, saluted stiffly the French Colonel who in turn did the same, although a little bewildered, and then I left the field proud but sad.

After a short rest I was looking for work, which was hard to find. I was a game warden for several large estates, was a tutor and traveling companion for a young wealthy count, and found finally a job in Düsseldorf where I sold carbon paper and ribbons for typewriters. The inflation crisis only got worse as it continued to spiral upwards. For example in spring, 1923, you got, for one American dollar, four billion Reichsmarks when, in more normal times, the rate of exchange had always been four mark, twenty pfennig for one dollar.

To illustrate this, I went one day to the post office to buy a stamp. A young man in front of me dropped one million marks on the floor. I tapped him on the shoulder and showed him his money. He looked down and smiled sadly and said, "I do not pick money up because the last time I picked up one million marks a button came off my pants and it cost me two million marks to have it sewn on and mind you one million marks used to be worth $250,000." The entire situation was ridiculously sad and in a way amusing. Of course there was madness and cunning in that scheme. The Reich could wipe out the tremendous internal debt with this cheap money and did so. Old people and pensioners were the ones who suffered the most.

At this time, I toyed with the idea of going to Russia and to find some kind of work flying there. But once again a lucky star led me to an American consulate in Leipzig. Here I met a young attaché from the United States. When I told him I was thinking of going to Russia he suggested instead that I should go to America and try my luck there. He issued me a passport, and I said goodbye to mother and to the Fatherland, boarded the old steamer "Yorck" in Bremerhafen and sailed in March, 1923, for the U.S.A. I felt like Columbus and looked forward to a new life in a new world.

Chapter 4 Photos

Left: My father (left) with his mother and his brother on one of his visits home, in Alhausen.

Bottom: My father's uncle Leonhard (left) and his son, ready for a day of hunting.

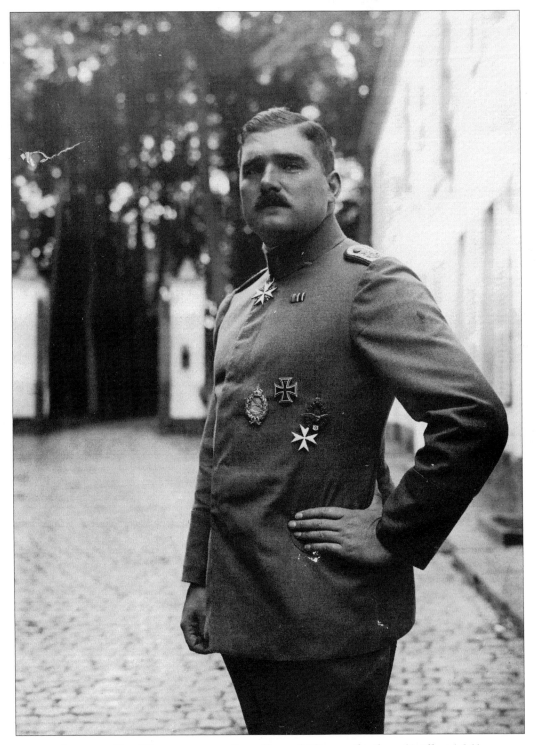

Count von Beroldingen, commanding officer of *Flieger-Abteilung (Artillerie) 261*,
picked up my father to take him to Écly to join his squadron.

Kulenkampff-Post wrote encouraging my father, since he was still recovering from his wounds, to join him at Haplincourt as his adjutant.

Kaiser Wilhelm II chats with a clergyman on a visit to the front on June 27, 1918.

A Zeppelin-Staaken "Giant" bomber.

An Albatros B.II in flight.

Flying during the First World War was a dangerous pursuit.

A pair of Friedrichshafen G.III bombers.

A Junkers D.I in a photo dated March 12, 1919, showing how advanced German aircraft design had become by the early Weimar period.

Amazingly, *Leutnant der Reserve* Mühlenbruch survived this crash.

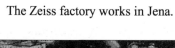

The Zeiss factory works in Jena.

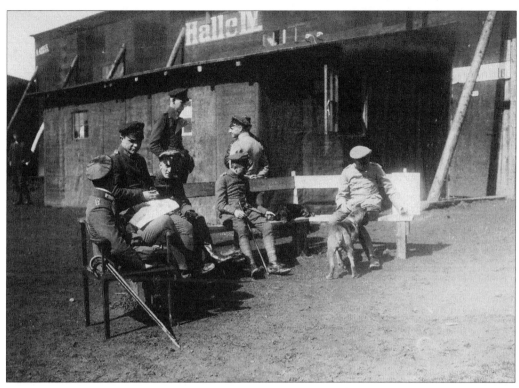

A moment of relaxation outside Halle IV at Écly airport.

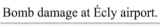
Bomb damage at Écly airport.

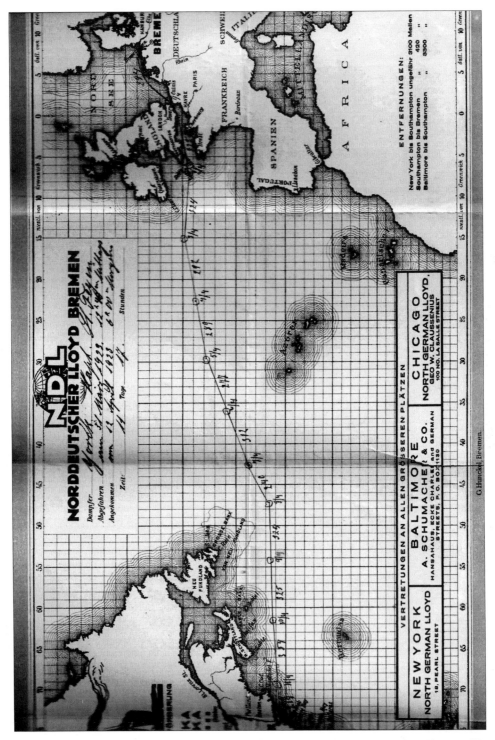

Document shows Rempe's route from Bremen to New York, March 1923 via "*The Yorck*".

Chapter 5

My Life in a New Country

Life on board the ship was new and interesting to me. After a few days the passengers got acquainted with each other and they all became a large family and fun chased away the thoughts of family, home and Fatherland. We saw the White Cliffs of Dover and passed England. The weather was fair first couple of days but then a storm came and grew stronger and stronger. We dropped anchor and spread bunker oil around the ship to calm the waves. Most people got sick, and I must say I felt a little uncomfortable myself, but the storm passed soon and we all had a wonderful time again. Finally we sighted land and our ship finally glided slowly into New York harbor pushed and pulled on by busy little tugboats. We could see the Statute of Liberty and the magnificent skyline of New York with its many skyscrapers. After a short time on Ellis Island with immigration people, I left my luggage on the dock and wandered through the streets; 42nd Street, Broadway,and Times Square, in a daze but happy. Late that night I went to the New York YMCA and fell into a long, long sleep dreaming of all sorts of things.

The next day I met a friendly cop who directed me to Rockaway Beach, Long Island, to a friend of his who owned and operated a greenhouse there. I was hired to take care and cut sweet peas and bring them in the early morning hours with a horse and wagon to the market. My pay was $8.00 and board per week. After three weeks I asked my boss for a raise. He asked me how much and I said ten. He said no, and I said I quit, he said no you don't quit, you're fired and there I was.

But next day, I had a new job for ten dollars per week washing dishes in a saloon. At that time I heard a voice saying "go West young man" and in five weeks as soon as I got my fare, I went West and came to Chicago. From there I went to Hershey, Illinois where my uncle, Reverend Joseph Rempe had a parish and where my sister, Margaret, was keeping house for him. I stayed there for a few days and worked there for a short time at the Paramount Knitting Mills in Kankakee making hosiery but left there for Chicago to do better things. Here I was again in this very big city looking for any kind of work. It's funny, but I felt I could do anything from running the city to a complicated engineering job, but nothing was available so I went to the outskirts and landed in Argo, Illinois.

Here was a tremendous big plant, the Illinois Corn Refining Company. The Director of Personnel told me that nothing was open except the position as a highly trained foreman for the sugar crystalline department. Since I was hungry and needed a job I told the Director I was just the man he was looking for and I was hired on the spot. My weekly wage was $72.80, which was a lot at that time and to me. I had forty men under me, including a very large black man who knew all there was to know about the job and kindly showed me what to do. So, with his help I caught on quickly with the work. The job was not hard but the hours were long, sixteen hours per day and seven days a week. Here I stayed for about one year when I felt I should change mostly for health reasons.

So back to Chicago I went and found a big amusement concern, Riverview Park. I was hired as a purchasing agent for $50.00 a week, but I had only six months to work and six months of vacation with pay. Here I spent the next three years until the owner died, and since I could not get along with his son, the next owner, I resigned with a savings of eight thousand dollars. I started to look around for my own business.

I met a guy who had the idea of getting rich quick. He persuaded me to go into business with him by building a roadhouse on the outskirts of Chicago, selling gasoline, meals, but most of all, liquor. The 1920's were the era of prohibition so of course selling liquor was not only illegal but dangerous. But we took that chance and built our roadhouse which we called "The Spanish Garden". It was on Rand Road, near Arlington Heights. I put all my savings into this risky enterprise but was uneasy all the time. Uneasy not only about breaking the law but also about my partner. We seemed to be very busy but did not appear to be making a profit. At one point I asked to examine the books and could see

that he was siphoning off the funds. I confronted him, he said he would pay it all back but instead disappeared from sight along with all my money; I never saw him or the money again.

Now I had to start all over, so I returned to Chicago and found a job as a salesman in a large department store selling pots and pans in the hardware section for twenty dollars per week. In two years my savings were about one thousand dollars again and, with the help of a friend I went to West Bend, Wisconsin, because I heard that community had a strong German element. I liked it there and so started my own paint business in the town and later added a gift area to my shop.

The next years were indeed very happy ones. West Bend is a wonderful city and the people were very friendly and I made many friends. My paint business prospered; finally I was my own boss. We had an airport near the city, and I organized a flying club and had my own plane. Sometimes I did skywriting to advertise my store's products. I also had a beautiful horse and a faithful motorcycle.

Almost every summer, I made an extended trip. In 1932 I went out West to the Grand Canyon. In 1933, I went to Yellowstone, and in 1934 I took my motorcycle to New York, put it on the boat and sailed to Europe. It was my first time back since 1923, and I saw my family as well as travelled throughout Europe including Russia on my motorcycle. These were wonderful years and therefore they went by very fast.

In 1937, I made an inventory of myself, I made a good living yes, but was in sort of a rut and getting along in years. I was looking in earnest for a wife and family. One day a man came along and offered to buy my paint store lock, stock and barrel, and I sold it then and there. I deposited the money in a bank, but took two thousand and changed them into travelers checks and went on a trip around the world. This trip, which had always been my secret wish, took me ten months to complete.

From West Bend I went to San Francisco, took a Japanese boat to Hawaii, stayed there one week and from there to Yokohama. I spent one month in Japan, and I found it delightful. Then on to Manila, Java, Sumatra, Hong Kong, Singapore, Ceylon, through the Suez Canal to Egypt. I spent two weeks there visiting the pyramids, the Sphinx and the amazing ruins at Luxor. By Christmas,1937, I was in Bethlehem and from there I went to Israel and then to Greece. From there it was on to Italy and, finally, to Germany where I stayed with my mother. But war clouds were clearly forming. I saw this in Italy when I heard Mussolini speak and it was even more clear when I saw the Nazi preparations for war under Hitler. I was anxious to return home to the United States and now my luckiest star intervened.

In April, 1938, I left my former homeland on the ship the "Bremen" and here fate played with me a lovely game. I met on this ship a man who was traveling with his wife to the United States to give lectures at different universities on German art and, in particular, on Albrecht Durer. His name was Dr. Haagen and he was a Professor of Art at the University of Munich. We became good friends and when we parted he promised to get in touch with me when he would get to Milwaukee.

I went back home to Wisconsin and started a new paint and gift store in Waukesha. I was barely in business when I received a letter from a Mrs. James Bach of Milwaukee inviting me to join her and her husband, Dr. James A. Bach, for dinner in honor of their house guest, Professor Haagen. I gladly accepted and met at the dinner their charming daughter, Catherine. I fell deeply in love with her, as the rest of you know. After a proper courtship and a wonderful summer we got married on November 8th, 1938. Amidst all that joy and happiness, it did not escape me that Germany had acknowledged defeat exactly twenty years previously to that very month. We had a lovely honeymoon in the Smokey Mountains and then moved into a brand new little place on the outskirts of Waukesha.

Fourteen months later, in January, 1940, our first child, Peter, was born. We then built our own house, modeled on German homes, on farm land we had purchased. Our second son, Paul, was born in April, 1942, as we were about to move into our new home. To make our lives perfect, our little daughter, Maria, arrived in October, 1945, and here we are all together and I hope for a long time.

But before I put down my pen and end this memoir, I want to give you, my children, some advice. I am sure you will always love your mother as there is no better person in the world. And I hope that when you walk through our woods you think of me sometimes. You three had a wonderful childhood here so remember that always and stick together come what may. My last advice, which you will find makes you a better person throughout your lives, it helped me to be happy helping others, is just one word. It is perhaps the most important word and it is compassion.

Certificate from the Chicago Board of Education showing Rempe passed the proficiency exam in English, 1925.

Flyer used by Rempe to promote his paint store in West Bend, circa 1930s

A Farewell to All!

Farewell--Adieu--Auf Wiedersehen to all my friends in West Bend
and Washington county. I say this
with deep and mingled emotions of
happiness and sorrow.

Happy, because I am starting on
a long journey, at the end of which
I will be again at the home of my
birth, gathered with the rest of my
family to celebrate the seventieth
birthday anniversary of "that wonderful mother of mine."

Sorry, because when I leave
this splendid community I am leaving
many real true friends who have been
very good to me, who have taken me
into their hearts and homes and who
have honored me with many of their
confidences--all of this I shall remember and cherish as long as I live.

So again I say Farewell--Adieu
--Auf Wiedersehen and knowing that I
will miss you all very much I am and
always hope to be

Your friend,

Leonhard R. Rempe

Rempe's 1937 farewell to all of his West Bend friends and patrons
announcing his travels around the world.

Family Photos

Picture of the four Rempe children: Karl standing; Margaret on the left;
Leonhard seated with whip; and Josephine on the right, circa 1898.

Rempe co-owned a roadhouse, The Spanish Gardens, in Arlington, Illinois during Prohibition.

Rempe owned and rode a horse in West Bend which recalled his riding days during World War I.

Rempe in his West Bend paint store.

Rempe at Deutsches Eck (German Corner) with his motorcycle, circa 1934. Note the U.S. flag on the handlebars of his cycle in contrast to the swastika on the monument.

Top: Rempe with his two sons, Paul and Peter in front of their German style home, mid-40s.

Bottom: Rempe with his three children, Maria, Paul and Peter, at the family farm.

Rempe's passport photo from his 1952 family trip to Europe.

Editor's Epilogue

Unpacking Memories in a New Country

What matters in life is not what
happens to you but what you
remember and how you
remember it.

— Gabriel Garcia Márquez,
Love in the Time of Cholera

Several issues raised by the 1956 memoir remain to be investigated. For example, how to account for the discrepancies between that memoir and the three preceding chapters? A quick answer, but ultimately wrong, would suggest that my father was not above telling a good story and that he was prepared to embellish the facts to achieve that end. Perhaps part of that answer would suggest the distance between his memoir and the events they describe led to inaccurate memories, or that he deliberately portrayed the war in a more positive light, allowing his memory to escape the ferocious fighting of the Eastern Front or the hazards of flight over the Western Front

But other questions persist. Given control over his material as the narrator in 1956, how did he wish to represent himself to his readers? What values did he wish to

signify and, more basically, why did he write what he did and didn't write what he didn't? For his "last testament," did my father rely only on his memory or did he consult the historical materials he saved and which have formed the basis of the first three chapters? Finally, ought the memoir be privileged over the historical documents because it gives voice to the subject, or should the archival sources be given pride of place because of their supposed objectivity? Should the memoir, chronologically last, have been placed first in the book because it gave voice to the author and allowed for a retrospective reflection on events which occurred over 40 years before? Or does it belong where placed because the first three chapters are based on solid historical evidence of certain past events and preserve in themselves an immediacy not available in the memoir?

The archival materials of the first three chapters bear evidentiary witness to past actuality, to events my father participated in and lived through; in a sense, they, and not my father, provide the record. It should not be a surprise that my father's 1956 recollections are not fully accurate representations of past actuality, but it cannot be asserted that his memoir is in any way less valid than the archival record. They are, in essence, two forms of truth and they most fundamentally raise the question, how are memory and history related?

In his very helpful book *History and Memory*, Dr Geoffrey Cubitt quotes George Santayana, who believed "History is nothing but assisted and recorded memory", John Lukas, who thinks of history as "the remembered past," and Peter Burke, who defines history "as social memory." On the other side of the argument, Dr Cubitt cites David Lowenthal, who writes: "History differs from memory not only in how knowledge of the past is acquired and validated but also in how it is transmitted, preserved and altered." Michael Bently asserts that "history is precisely non-memory, a systematic discipline which seeks to rely on mechanisms and controls quite different from those which memory triggers and often intended to give memory the lie."[1]

Cubitt continues his examination of the difference between history and memory by quoting the English historian and philosopher R. G. Collingwood. Collingwood argued that while history was based on verifiable evidence, memory was completely subjective since it had no point of reference "outside the personal consciousness of the rememberer."[2] On the other hand, the German historian and philosopher Wilhelm Dilthey insisted on the validity of autobiographical remembering and concluded:

> The person who seeks the connecting threads in the history of his life, from different points of view, created a coherence in that life which he is now putting into words. He has created it by experiencing values and realizing purposes in his life, making plans for it, seeing his past in terms of development

and his future as the shaping of his life and of whatever he values most.[3]

This idea of memory functioning in an interpretative and selective way to provide meaning to one's life is also developed by Jacques Le Goff, who writes: "memory on which history draws and which it nourishes in return, seeks to save the past in order to secure the present and the future."[4]

Paul Fussell is more direct in stating that we expect a memoir dealing with a great historical event to "dramatize things."[5] But then, bowing to memory, he quotes historian Robert Kee, who asserted: "no wonder it is those artists who recreate life rather than try to re-capture it who, in one way, prove the good historians in the end."[6]

The historian David Taylor has no difficulty in accepting that memories are of interest to the historian, even though he acknowledges that "rather than being indisputably accurate, memories are constructed, contaminated and subject to manipulation."[7] Taylor reminds us that "memory is something that is constructed from the vantage point of the present."[8] Cubitt put the point forcefully when he wrote: "everything that happens when we remember the past happens in a present from which the past is absent."[9] Taylor argues that remembering, or the process of creative retrieval, is influenced by the present moment in which the retrieved is taking place and therefore cannot be identical to the original memory: "In that sense, each remembrance of an event is new and distinct from the earlier remembrance, let alone from the event itself." Nevertheless, Taylor argues, although perhaps factually inaccurate the value of the memory in its own terms is not negated.[10]

My father's 1930 and 1956 memoirs provide good examples of Dr Taylor's point. The 1930 memoir, unfortunately unfinished, was written in German within seven years of his arrival in New York. This memoir describes an intense night fight against Russian forces who stormed the German defensive wire. The terrors of the battle are described with an immediacy quite absent from his 1956 memoir, which was written in English. Taylor might well conclude that while my father's two memoirs offer differing perspectives on the war, they were "equally right (or wrong) at the time of recollecting and recounting."[11]

Even though narratives based on memory are constructed and clearly change depending upon the time in which they were written, Taylor argues that such narratives have value because they provide a means of dealing with present problems and they help make "sensible and coherent the seeming chaos of human existence."[12] For Taylor, the actual process of individual or autobiographical memory works to emphasize certain events while de-emphasizing others or even forgetting altogether parts of an individual past. This selective retelling ultimately works to provide a "meaningful and present narrative."[13]

In common with the process of researching, interpreting, and writing history, memory is not value free or entirely objective because the encoding of the initial experience and its later recall do not occur in a vacuum. They are always impacted by present beliefs, under-standings, and values. But even if the end product of memory is constructed, selective and manipulated, Taylor argues that "consideration of falsifications and distortion are largely beside the point."[14] Professor Geoffrey Cubitt, quoting Sir Richard Bartlett, agrees: "remembering is hardly ever really accurate and it is not at all important that it should be so."[15]

The importance of memory is that its narrative use defines us, as we employ memories to give meaning and validity to our lives. As such, autobiographical narratives anchored in memory help to integrate past, present, and future to create a more stable self-identity. As Taylor has it, "the narrative telling of who we were is not the same as telling of the past as it actually was but rather is a selective process that highlights aspects of the past that are (or seem to be) significant in the present time of retelling."[16] Taylor reaches an important conclusion when he points out that "greater attention needs to be paid to the time of writing and the issues that were important to the writer at that time than to the past described."[17]

If this be the case, a closer examination of his 1956 memoir might reveal what values my father wished to impart, how he wanted to represent himself and why discrepancies exist between the memoir and the documented historical record. Undoubtedly aware of his failing health, he wrote it aged 63 when nearing the statistical mortality rate of that time. In 1956 he could contemplate a good life on both sides of the Atlantic. In his adopted country he maintained his practice of saving historical evidence for a personal archive. While he did not include these documented facts within his memoir, preferring to use the majority of his handwritten pages to relate his wartime experiences, he could reflect on his achievements from his arrival at Ellis Island, via the passenger ship *The Yorck* in the spring of 1923. Just 30, he spent some time on Long Island, NY before moving to Illinois to be with his sister. He left Chicago for West Bend, Wisconsin, a city he understood to have had a significant German population. There he became a successful owner of a paint store and he continued his interest in flying as he became president of the West Bend flying club and helped establish the airport in that city.

In 1937 he sold his store in order to fulfill a dream of traveling around the world. Returning after several months of travel, he settled in Waukesha, Wisconsin in 1938 and in that year, at age 45, he married a lovely and intelligent woman from Milwaukee. During World War II, my father worked in a local industrial plant making war-related materials and this decade also saw the birth of his three children. In 1956, he could take some satisfaction over the German-style home he helped build and over the farm he owned.

As he faced an uncertain future he dedicated his memoir, his last testament, to his family. Sixteen of the twenty-four pages in a small notebook concern the 1914–23 period. These pages appear, unedited, in Chapter 4. Looking back from a perspective of over 40 years, it should not surprise us that the war years appear as more "romanticized" than they do in the 1930 memoir or in the historical documents he saved; his view of the war changed as his circumstances changed.

Unlike those contemporaries who wrote of a futile and senseless war, his memoir describes a war that was justified and fought as a matter of honor. He recollects a war where simple luck rather than personal heroics allowed him to survive. His 1956 view of the First World War was one of comradeship rather than bloody slaughter and severe hardship. The narrative stress is not on "blood and mud" but on discipline and duty; not on a fool's courage but on genuine valor. The memoir reveals little disillusionment, nor much about his participation in several savage battles on the Eastern Front, nor about the stress and strain of high-altitude flying over the Western Front. His memory recalled a war rather different from the one in which he fought. His narrative expresses few regrets—victory several times within Germany's grasp, but ultimately defeat in an honorable cause.

The cultural historian Jay Winter writes that the marked brutality of the First World War survived the conflict and became a distinguishing characteristic of the postwar world. However, Professor Winter balances that assessment with a more positive outlook as he acknowledges that "compassion was there too and deserves to be recognized as an essential component in the recovery from the war."[18] The last word written by my father for his 1956 memoir was the advice he gave to his children: "to have compassion."

Appendix

Commendations for Military Service

Iron Cross Second Class,
(awarded October 17, 1915)

Pilot's Badge
(*Flugzeugführer- abzeichen*)
(awarded October 13, 1917)

Iron Cross First Class
(awarded March 23, 1918)

Wound Badge
(*Verwundeten-abzeichen*)
(awarded August, 1918)

Young Pilots Memorial Award,
1917–1921
(awarded 1922)

German Commemorative
Medallion of the World War
(no date)

Two letters also bear notice. The first, by the District Commander at Paderborn, Konig (parts of which appear in the text), testifies to *Leutnant der Reserve* Rempe's "active military service from November 20, 1914 until September 21, 1919." Konig's letter, dated September 26, 1921, speaks of Rempe's presence at the battles of Mlawa, Kupischki, Schimanzi, Ponedeli, Birshy and Dünaburg, and Konig writes of additional conflict at Postwai, battles between lakes Boginskoje and Driswiaty and major battles between lakes Naroch and Oriewiety.

The second letter is from Captain Victor Krocker of District Command VI, previously leader of *Flieger-Abteilung 423.* Captain Krocker writes:

Lieutenant of the Reich, Leonhard Rempe served as a pilot in the *Flieger-Abteilung 423.* (i.e. the *Artillerie-Fliegerstaffel 116*) from January–October 1919.

During this time, he completed numerous flights in service to the Weimar Republic, showing outstanding abilities even in very difficult weather and material conditions. His vast experience on the front during the campaign was particularly helpful. He successfully flew both one-seaters (Fokker D. VII, Alb. D.V.) and two seaters (L.V.G., and C.VI, Rubild), and demonstrated complete confidence.

In the technical realm, his knowledge also made him valuable to the Staffel as a "technical officer." He was always reliable and won friends everywhere through his care and dedication.

In both military and social settings, he was a much beloved comrade . . .

Endnotes

Introduction

Keegan, John, *The First World* (New York: Alfred A. Knopf, 1999), p. 303.

Rempe Papers, May 3, 1935.

Morrow, John H. Jr., *The Great War: An Imperial History* (London: Routledge, 2004), p. 21.

Chapter 1

1. Rempe Papers, 1930 memoir.
2. Rempe Papers, 1930 memoir.
3. Rempe Papers, August 5, 1914.
4. Rempe Papers, August 10, 1914.
5. Rempe Papers, 1930 memoir.
6. Rempe Papers, 1930 memoir.
7. Rempe Papers, August 15, 1914.
8. Cron, Hermann (trans. Colton, C. F.), *Imperial German Army 1914–1918: Organization, Structure, Orders of Battle* (Solihull: Helion and Co., 2002), Kindle e-book.
9. "German Army (German Empire)" https:// en. wikipedia.Org/wiki/ German_ Army_ (German _Empire) accessed 2015.
10. Stone, Norman, *The Eastern Front 1914- 1917*, 2nd ed. (London: Penguin Books, 1998), pp. 171–72.
11. Wikipedia [website], "Army of the Niemen" http://en.wikipedia.org/wiki/Army_of_the_ Niemen; History of War [website], "General Otto von Below, 1857–1944" www.historyof war.org/articles/people_below_otto.html; accessed 2015.
12. Ives, Walter E., "Will Germany Attack Russia's Bread Line?," The *New York Times*, May 5, 1915.
13. Rempe Papers, 1930 memoir.
14. Gentleman's Military Interest Club [web- site], "The Niemen Army attacks in 1915" http:// gmic.co.uk accessed 2015.
15. Gentleman's Military Interest Club [web- site], "The Niemen Army attacks in 1915" http:// gmic.co.uk accessed 2015.
16. Gentleman's Military Interest Club [web- site], "The Niemen Army attacks in 1915" http://gmic.co.uk accessed 2015; Rempe Papers: a letter, dated September 26, 1921, from Konig, the District Commander in Paderborn, testifying to Leonhard Rempe's military service

at Kupischki. See the Appendix in this work for the full text of this letter.

17. Rempe Papers, 1930 memoir.
18. Rempe Papers. There are no dates on the maps and sites of combat he underlined.
19. Rempe Papers: letter from the District Commander in Paderborn, September 26, 1921.
20. Rempe Papers, October 20, 1915.
21. Rempe Papers, October 18, 1915.
22. Rempe Papers, 1930 and 1956 memoirs.
23. Rempe Papers, 1930 memoir.
24. Rempe Papers, 1930 memoir.
25. Morrow, *The Great War: An Imperial History*, p. 21.
26. Keegan, *The First World*, p. 303.
27. Stone, *The Eastern Front 1914-1911*, p. 231.
28. Keegan, *The First World* , p. 303.
29. Stone, *The Eastern Front 1914-1911*, pp. 230–31.
30. Stone, *The Eastern Front 1914- 1911*, p. 230.
31. Herwig, Holger H., *The First World War: Germany and Austria–Hungary 1914–1918* (London: Arnold, 1997), p. 267.
32. Stone, *The Eastern Front 1914- 1911*, pp. 228–29.
33. Rempe Papers, 1930 memoir.
34. Herwig, *The First World War: Germany and Austria–Hungary 1914–1918*, p. 207.
35. Herwig, 1997, p. 207; Stone, 1998, p. 231.
36. Hart, Peter, *The Great War: A Combat History of the First World War* (Oxford: Oxford University Press, 2013), p. 243.
37. Tunstall, Graydon A., "Austria–Hungary and the Brusilov Offensive of 1916," *The Historian*, 70:1 (spring 2008), p. 52; Keegan, *The First World*, pp. 305–06.
38. Herwig, *The First World War: Germany and Austria–Hungary 1914–1918*, pp. 209–15.
39. Rempe Papers, 1930 memoir.
40. Rempe Papers, 1930 memoir.
41. Rempe Papers: letter from the District Commander in Paderborn, September 26, 1921.
42. Thomas, Nigel and Bujeiro, Ramiro, *The German Army in World War I: 1915–17, Men-at-Arms 407* (Oxford: Osprey Publishing Ltd, 2004), pp. 5–6.
43. Rempe Papers, November 18, 1916.

Chapter 2

1. Rempe Papers, 1956 memoir.

2. Rempe Papers, November 8, 1916.
3. Rempe Papers, November 18, 1916.
4. Rempe Papers, 1956 memoir.
5. Rempe Papers, 1956 memoir; *Wikipedia* [website], "Prince Friedrich Karl of Prussia (1893–1917)" https://en.wiki pedia.org/wiki/ Prince_Friedrich_Karl_of_Prussia_(1893–1917), accessed 2015.
6. Hoeppner, Ernst von (trans. Hawley Larned, J.), *Germany's War in the Air: The Development and Operations of German Military Aviation in the World War* (Nashville: The Battery Press, 1994), p. 36.
7. Rempe Papers, 1956 memoir.
8. Rempe Papers, Flight Log Book 1916–1917.
9. British General Staff. *Handbook of German Military and Naval Aviation (War) 1914–1918* (Nashville: The Battery Press, 1995), p. 21.
10. *Handbook of German Military and Naval Aviation (War) 1914–1918*, pp. 19–25.
11. Foreword to Grosz, Peter M., *Rumpler C.IV*, Windsock Datafile No. 35 (Hertfordshire: Albatros Productions, 1992).
12. Morrow, John H., Jr, *The Great War in the Air: Military Aviation from 1909 to 1921* (Washington D.C.: Smithsonian Institution Press, 1993), p. 220.
13. Morrow, John H., Jr, "The War in the Air," in Strachan, Hew (ed.), The *Oxford Illustrated History of the First World War* (Oxford: Oxford University Press, 1998), p. 276.
14. Grosz, *Rumpler C.IV*, pp. 2–3.
15. Rimell, Ray, *Rumpler C.IV at War*, Windsock Datafile No. 149 (Hertfordshire: Albatros Productions, 2011).
16. Grosz, *Rumpler C.IV*, p. 7; Hoeppner, *Germany's War in the Air: The Development and Operations of German Military Aviation in the World War*, pp. 18–20.
17. Morrow, *The Great War in the Air: Military Aviation from 1909 to 1921*, p. 198.
18. Grosz, *Rumpler C.IV*, p. 4.
19. Morrow, *The Great War in the Air: Military Aviation from 1909 to 1921*, p. 299; Grosz, *Rumpler C.IV*, pp. 5–6.
20. Hoeppner, *Germany's War in the Air: The Development and Operations of German Military Aviation in the World War*, pp. 18–20; p. 82.
21. Cron, 2002, Kindle e-book; Rempe Papers, no date.
22. Hoeppner, *Germany's War in the Air: The Development and Operations of German Military Aviation in the World War*, p. 39.
23. Morrow, *The Great War in the Air: Military Aviation from 1909 to 1921*, p. 346.
24. firstworldwar.com [website], "The War in the Air—Observation and Reconnaissance," by Unikoski, Ari, http://www.firstworldwar. com/airwar/observation.htm accessed 2015.
25. Hoeppner, *Germany's War in the Air: The Development and Operations of German Military Aviation in the World War*, p. 99.
26. Hoeppner, *Germany's War in the Air: The Development and Operations of German Military Aviation in the World War*, p. 73.
27. *Handbook of German Military and Naval Aviation (War) 1914–1918*, p. 55.
28. *Handbook of German Military and Naval Aviation (War) 1914–1918*, p. 55.
29. Morrow, *The Great War in the Air: Military Aviation from 1909 to 1921*, p. 230.
30. Hoeppner, *Germany's War in the Air: The Development and Operations of German Military Aviation in the World War*, p. 99.
31. Hoeppner, *Germany's War in the Air: The Development and Operations of German Military Aviation in the World War*, p. 99.
32. *Handbook of German Military and Naval Aviation (War) 1914–1918*, p. 35; Morrow, *The Great War in the Air: Military Aviation from 1909 to 1921*, p. 230.
33. Grosz, *Rumpler C.IV*, pp. 6–7.
34. Rempe Papers, "Flight Reports," September 18, 1917.
35. Rempe Papers, "Barograph Reading"; Grosz, *Rumpler C.IV*, pp. 5–6.
36. Morrow, *The Great War in the Air: Military Aviation from 1909 to 1921*, p. 299.
37. Morrow, *The Great War in the Air: Military Aviation from 1909 to 1921*, p. 347.
38. Rempe Papers, "Flight Reports," September 30, 1917.
39. Rempe Papers, "Flight Reports," December 11, 1917; January 25, 1918; January 29, 1918. In his Papers, unfortunately undated, my father has a drawing of a matchbox showing on its cover a handwritten promise that, "I shall not have another cigarette until I have shot down another SPAD."
40. Rempe Papers, "Flight Reports," September 10, 1917; September 22, 1917; September 25, 1917; October 1, 1917.
41. Rempe Papers, "Flight Reports," October 17, 1917.
42. Rempe Papers, "Flight Reports," October 13, 1917.
43. Rempe Papers, "Flight Reports," December 10, 1917.
44. Morrow, "The War in the Air," pp. 275–76.
45. Rempe Papers, January 6, 1918.
46. Rempe Papers, letters dated September 19, 1938; January 6, 1918.

47. Rempe Papers, dinner menus from December 15, 1917 and December 24, 1917.
48. Rempe Papers, playbills for February 10 and 14, 1918. In his classic study *The Great War and Modern Memory* (Oxford: Oxford University Press, 1975), Paul Fussell writes about the many ironies of war. Certainly this is a great example of that phenomenon— military units seated in a theater in the midst of a theater of war to watch a play about the rape of the Sabine women.
49. Rempe Papers, March 10, 1918.
50. Keegan, *The First World* , pp. 292–93.
51. Hoeppner, *Germany's War in the Air: The Development and Operations of German Military Aviation in the World War*, p. 147.
52. Herwig, Holger H. and Heyman, Neil M., *Biographical Dictionary of World War I* (Westport, CN: Greenwood Press, 1982), p. 22.
53. Fussell, *The Great War and Modern Memory*, p. 17.
54. Morrow, *The Great War in the Air: Military Aviation from 1909 to 1921*, pp. 201–02.
55. Rempe Papers, 1956 memoir.
56. Rempe Papers, March 21, 1918; March 23, 1918.
57. Rempe Papers, June 3, 1918; Keegan, *The First World*, p. 397.
58. Rempe Papers, June 7, 1918.
59. Rempe Papers, June 7, 1918.
60. *Wikipedia* [website], "Third Battle of the Aisne" https://en.wikipedia.org/wiki/Third_Battle_of_the_Aisne accessed 2015.
61. Rempe Papers, letter from Dr Hermann Kulenkampff-Post, June 24, 1918.
62. Rempe Papers, undated.
63. Rempe Papers, August 9, 1918.
64. Rempe Papers, September 15, 1918.
65. Keegan, *The First World*, p. 409.
66. Keegan, *The First World*, p. 419.
67. Herwig and Heyman, *Biographical Dictionary of World War I*, p. 138.
68. Rempe Papers, November 13, 1918.
69. Rempe Papers, November 23, 1918.

Chapter 3

1. Herwig and Heyman, *Biographical Dictionary of World War I*, p. 172.
2. Eyck, Erich, *A History of the Weimar Republic* (Hoboken, NJ: John Wiley and Sons, 1967), p. 51.
3. Eyck, *A History of the Weimar Republic*, p. 41.
4. Gay, Peter, *Weimar Culture: The Outsider as Insider* (New York: Norton and Co., 1969), pp. 17–18.
5. Jones, Nigel, *Hitler's Heralds: The Story of the Freikorps 1918–1922* (New York: Dorset Press, 1987).
6. Scott, Ben, "The Origins of the Freikorps: A Re-evaluation," *The University of Sussex Journal of Contemporary History*, 1 (2000), p. 4.
7. Watt, Richard M., *The Kings Depart: The Tragedy of Germany, Versailles and the German Revolution* (New York: Simon and Schuster, 1968), p. 509.
8. Watt, *The Kings Depart: The Tragedy of Germany, Versailles and the German Revolution*, p. 251.
9. Watt, *The Kings Depart: The Tragedy of Germany, Versailles and the German Revolution*, p. 296.
10. Gordon, Harold J., *The Reichswehr and the German Republic, 1919–1926* (Princeton: Princeton University Press, 1957), p. 60.
11. Gordon, *The Reichswehr and the German Republic, 1919–1926*, pp. 59–60.
12. Waite, Robert G. L., *Vanguard of Nazism: The Free Corps Movement in Postwar Germany 1918–1923*, 2nd ed. (New York: Norton and Co., 1969), p. 13.
13. Waite, *Vanguard of Nazism: The Free Corps Movement in Postwar Germany 1918–1923*, p. 35.
14. Rempe Papers, 1919.
15. Jones, *Hitler's Heralds: The Story of the Freikorps 1918–1922*, p. 51.
16. Jones, *Hitler's Heralds: The Story of the Freikorps 1918–1922*, p. 52.
17. Rempe Papers, December 18, 1918.
18. Scott, 2000, p. 5.
19. Watt, *The Kings Depart: The Tragedy of Germany, Versailles and the German Revolution*, p. 248.
20. Waite, *Vanguard of Nazism: The Free Corps Movement in Postwar Germany 1918–1923*, p. 34.
21. Jones, *Hitler's Heralds: The Story of the Freikorps 1918–1922*, p. 50.
22. Gordon, *The Reichswehr and the German Republic, 1919–1926*, p. 37.
23. Waite, *Vanguard of Nazism: The Free Corps Movement in Postwar Germany 1918–1923*, p. 29.
24. Waite, *Vanguard of Nazism: The Free Corps Movement in Postwar Germany 1918–1923*, p. 36.
25. Jones, *Hitler's Heralds: The Story of the Freikorps 1918–1922*, pp. 58–61.
26. Rempe Papers, 1956 memoir.
27. Rempe Papers, 1956 memoir.
28. Waldman, Eric, *The Spartacist Uprising of 1919 and the Crisis of the German Socialist Movement* (Milwaukee: Mar- quette University Press, 1958), p. 196.

29. Angress, Werner T., *Stillborn Revolution: The Communist Bid for Power in Germany, 1921–1923* (Princeton: Prince- ton University Press, 1963), p. 476.

30. Rempe Papers, January 13, 1919.

31. Rempe Papers, January 18, 1919.

32. Rempe Papers, January 22, 1919.

33. Jones, *Hitler's Heralds: The Story of the Freikorps 1918–1922*, p. 79.

34. Rempe Papers, February 3, 1919.

35. Rempe Papers, February 22, 1919.

36. Jones, *Hitler's Heralds: The Story of the Freikorps 1918–1922*, pp. 83–85.

37. Schumann, Dirk (trans. Dunlap, Thomas), *Political Violence in the Weimar Republic 1918–1933: Fight for the Streets and Fear of Civil War* (New York: Berghahn Books, 2009), p. 9.

38. Rempe Papers, March 5, 1919.

39. Rempe Papers, March 6 and March 15, 1919.

40. Rempe Papers, no date.

41. Jones, *Hitler's Heralds: The Story of the Freikorps 1918–1922*, p. 86.

42. Rempe Papers, April 2, 1919.

43. Rempe Papers, April 12 and April 14, 1919.

44. Rempe Papers, May 9, 1919.

45. Rempe Papers, May 17 and June 10, 1919.

46. Rempe Papers, June 24, 1919.

47. Rempe Papers, July 8, 1919.

48. Rempe Papers, July 29, 1919.

49. Rempe Papers, September 20, 1919.

50. Rempe Papers, September 27, 1919.

51. Rempe Papers, March 22, 1920.

52. Rempe Papers, November, 26, 1920.

53. Rempe Papers, June 4, 1921.

54. Rempe Papers, 1956 memoir.

Chapter 4

1. Once upon a time . . . This is how all fairy tales start.

2. *West Prussian Field Artillery Regiment No. 35*.

3. An anatomical term collectively describing the annular arrangement of lymphoid tissue in the pharynx.

4. The actual date was November 18, 1916.

5. *Flieger-Abteilung* (Artillerie) 261.

6. The actual date was March 21, 1918, the first day of Ludendorff's great offensive in the West, Operation Michael.

7. Georges Guynemer was killed in action on September 11, 1917.

8. The actual date was January 15, 1919.

Chapter 5

1. Cubitt, Geoffrey, *History and Memory* (Manchester: Manchester University Press, 2007), p. 31.

2. Cubitt, *History and Memory*, p. 33.

3. Cubitt, *History and Memory*, p. 34.

4. Le Goff, Jacques (trans. Rendall, Steven and Claman, Elizabeth), *History and Memory* (New York: Columbia University Press, 1992), p. 99.

5. Fussell, *The Great War and Modern Memory*, p. 205.

6. Fussell, *The Great War and Modern Memory*, p. 311.

7. Taylor, David, *Memory, Narrative and The Great War: Rifleman Patrick MacGill and the Construction of Wartime Experience* (Liverpool: Liverpool University Press, 2013), p. 48.

8. Taylor, *Memory, Narrative and The Great War: Rifleman Patrick MacGill and the Construction of Wartime Experience*, p. 79.

9. Cubitt, *History and Memory*, p. 78.

10. Taylor, *Memory, Narrative and The Great War: Rifleman Patrick MacGill and the Construction of Wartime Experience*, p. 49.

11. Taylor, *Memory, Narrative and The Great War: Rifleman Patrick MacGill and the Construction of Wartime Experience*, p. 260.

12. Taylor, *Memory, Narrative and The Great War: Rifleman Patrick MacGill and the Construction of Wartime Experience*, pp. 56–57.

13. Taylor, *Memory, Narrative and The Great War: Rifleman Patrick MacGill and the Construction of Wartime Experience*, p. 57.

14. Taylor, *Memory, Narrative and The Great War: Rifleman Patrick MacGill and the Construction of Wartime Experience*, p. 57.

15. Cubitt, *History and Memory*, p. 79.

16. Taylor, *Memory, Narrative and The Great War: Rifleman Patrick MacGill and the Construction of Wartime Experience*, p. 54.

17. Taylor, *Memory, Narrative and The Great War: Rifleman Patrick MacGill and the Construction of Wartime Experience*, p. 57.

18. Winter, Jay, *Sites of Memory, Sites of Mourning: The Great War in European Cultural History* (Cambridge: Cambridge University Press, 1995), p. 6.

Bibliography

Primary Sources

Papers of Leonhard R. Rempe, 1914–21.

Log Book from Flight School Hundsfeld, November 25, 1916 to February 7, 1917. The log gives information on 85 training flights during this period.

Fourteen Flight Reports from September 10, 1917 to January 29, 1918.

Papers numbering to 130, which include military orders, maps, hunting permits, military awards and commendations etc., 1914–21.

Incomplete memoir written in German in 1930.

Memoir written in English in 1956.

1914–20 photographs from Leonhard Rempe's photo album.

Secondary Sources

Angress, Werner T., *Stillborn Revolution: The Communist Bid for Power in Germany, 1921–1923* (Princeton: Princeton University Press, 1963)

British General Staff. *Handbook of German Military and Naval Aviation (War) 1914–1918* (Nashville: The Battery Press, 1995)

Buttar, Prit, *Collision of Empires: The War on the Eastern Front in 1914* (Oxford: Osprey Publishing, 2014), Kindle e-book

Carsten, F. L., *The Reichswehr and Politics, 1918–1933* (Berkeley: University of California Press, 1973)

Chickering, Roger, *Imperial Germany and the Great War*, 2nd ed. (Cambridge: Cambridge University Press, 2004)

Cron, Hermann (trans. Colton, C. F.), *Imperial German Army 1914–1918: Organization, Structure, Orders of Battle* (Solihull: Helion and Co., 2002), Kindle e-book

Cubitt, Geoffrey, *History and Memory* (Manchester: Manchester University Press, 2007)

Eyck, Erich, *A History of the Weimar Republic* (Hoboken, NJ: John Wiley and Sons, 1967)

Fussell, Paul, *The Great War and Modern Memory* (Oxford: Oxford Univ. Press, 1975)

Gay, Peter, *Weimar Culture: The Outsider as Insider* (New York: Norton and Co., 1969)

Gilbert, Martin, *The First World War: A Complete History* (New York: Henry Holt, 1994)

Gordon, Harold J., *The Reichswehr and the German Republic, 1919–1926* (Princeton: Princeton University Press, 1957)

Grosz, Peter M., *Rumpler C.IV*, Windsock Datafile No. 35 (Hertfordshire: Albatros Productions, 1992)

Hart, Peter, *The Great War: A Combat History of the First World War* (Oxford: Oxford University Press, 2013)

Heiber, Helmut (trans. Yuill, W. E.), *The Weimar Republic* (Oxford: Blackwell, 1993)

Herwig, Holger H. and Heyman, Neil M., *Biographical Dictionary of World War I* (Westport, CN: Greenwood Press, 1982)

Herwig, Holger H., *The First World War: Germany and Austria–Hungary 1914–1918* (London: Arnold, 1997)

Histories of Two Hundred and Fifty-One Divisions of the German Army which participated in the War (1914–1918) (Washington: Government Printing Office, 1920)

Hoeppner, Ernst von (trans. Hawley Larned, J.), *Germany's War in the Air: The Development and Operations of German Military Aviation in the World War (Nashville: The Battery Press, 1994)*

Ives, Walter E., "Will Germany Attack Russia's Bread Line?", *The New York Times*, May 5, 1915

Jones, Nigel, *Hitler's Heralds: The Story of the Freikorps 1918–1922* (New York: Dorset Press, 1987)

Keegan, John, *The First World War* (New York: Alfred A. Knopf, 1999)

Le Goff, Jacques (trans. Rendall, Steven and Claman, Elizabeth), *History and Memory* (New York: Columbia University Press, 1992)

Morrow, John H., Jr, *The Great War in the Air: Military Aviation from 1909 to 1921* (Washington D.C.: Smithsonian Institution Press, 1993)

——, "The War in the Air," in Strachan, Hew (ed.), *The Oxford Illustrated History of the First World War* (Oxford: Oxford University Press, 1998)

——, *The Great War: An Imperial History* (London: Routledge, 2003)

Mosse, George, *Fallen Soldiers: Reshaping the Memory of the World Wars* (Oxford: Oxford University Press, 1990)

Neiberg, Michael and Jordan, David, *History of World War I: The Eastern Front 1914–1920* (London: Amber Books, 2003), Kindle e-book

Rimell, Ray, *Rumpler C.IV at War*, Windsock Datafile No. 149 (Hertfordshire: Albatros Productions, 2011)

Root, Irving G., *Battles East: A History of the Eastern Front in the First World War* (Baltimore: Publish America, 2007)

Schumann, Dirk (trans. Dunlap, Thomas), *Political Violence in the Weimar Republic 1918–1933: Fight for the Streets and Fear of Civil War* (New York: Berghahn Books, 2009), p. 9.

Scott, Ben, "The Origins of the Freikorps: A Re-evaluation," *The University of Sussex Journal of Contemporary History*, 1 (2000)

Stone, Norman, *The Eastern Front 1914–1917*, 2nd ed. (London: Penguin Books, 1998)

Taylor, David, *Memory, Narrative and The Great War: Rifleman Patrick MacGill and the Construction of Wartime Experience* (Liverpool: Liverpool University Press, 2013)

Thomas, Nigel and Bujeiro, Ramiro, *The German Army in World War I: 1915–17*, Men-at-Arms 407 (Oxford: Osprey Publishing Ltd, 2004).

Tucker, Spencer C., *The Great War 1914–1918* (Bloomington: Indiana University Press, 1998)

Tunstall, Graydon A., "Austria–Hungary and the Brusilov Offensive of 1916," *The Historian*, 70:1 (spring 2008)

Waite, Robert G. L., *Vanguard of Nazism: The Free Corps Movement in Postwar Germany 1918–1923*, 2nd ed. (New York: Norton and Co., 1969)

Waldman, Eric, *The Spartacist Uprising of 1919 and the Crisis of the German Socialist Movement* (Milwaukee: Marquette University Press, 1958)

Watt, Richard M., *The Kings Depart: The Tragedy of Germany, Versailles and the German Revolution* (New York: Simon and Schuster, 1968)

Winter, Jay, *Sites of Memory, Sites of Mourning: The Great War in European Cultural History* (Cambridge: Cambridge University Press, 1995)

Websites

firstworldwar.com [website], "The War in the Air – Observation and Reconnaissance," by Unikoski, Ari, www.firstworldwar.com/airwar/observation.htm accessed 2015

Gentleman's Military Interest Club [website], "The Niemen Army attacks in 1915" http://gmic.co.uk accessed 2015

History of War [website], "General Otto von Below, 1857–1944"www.historyofwar.org/articles/people_below_otto.html accessed 2015

Wikipedia [website], "Army of the Niemen" http://en.wikipedia.org/wiki/Army_of_the_Niemen accessed 2015

Wikipedia [website], "German Army (German Empire)" https://en.wikipedia.org/wiki/German_Army_(German_Empire) accessed 2015

Wikipedia [website], "Prince Friedrich Karl of Prussia (1893–1917)" https://en.wikipedia.org/wiki/Prince_Friedrich_Karl_of_Prussia_(1893–1917) accessed 2015

Wikipedia [website], "Third Battle of the Aisne" https://en.wikipedia.org/wiki/Third_Battle_of_the_Aisne accessed 2015

Index

Photo List

About the Author

Paul L. Rempe earned B.A. and M.A. degrees in History at Marquette University in Milwaukee. He continued his graduate studies at Stony Brook University in New York, where he received a Ph.D. in History. During his time at Carroll University in Waukesha, Wisconsin, Dr. Rempe taught a variety of history courses and published a number of articles and book reviews in his academic discipline of British and Irish history.

Now retired, he and his wife enjoy spending time with their three sons and grandchildren while still taking time to write and to travel.